PAUL OF TARSUS

HIS GOSPEL AND LIFE

PAUL OF TARSUS

HIS GOSPEL AND LIFE

HEROLD WEISS

Andrews University Press
Berrien Springs, MI 49104

© 1986

92 91 90 89 88 87 86   7 6 5 4 3 2 1

ISBN 0-943872-27-8
Library of Congress catalog card number 86-072148

This Book is Dedicated

to

HEROLD EDUARDO *and* CARLOS ORVAL

Who are reading the ancient texts

with the questions of the next generation

TABLE OF CONTENTS

PREFACE

A quick review of the Pauline shelf in any library reveals a surprising gap. There are many excellent erudite monographs dealing with some aspect of Paul's thought, or general introductions written for specialists. On the other hand, there are popular books of a devotional nature written with lay persons in mind, but which inform the reader mainly about the issues that seem to be relevant at the moment. This book has been written in order to bridge this gap. It adresses the non-specialist who wishes to know the apostle Paul in terms of the issues that he had to face. Hopefully reading this book will serve to open-up the apostle's world so as to encourage further study of his own letters.

This is a book about someone by someone else. It is inevitable that some distortion may have occurred as the life and the thought of Paul was being processed through another mind. But it has been a conscious effort on my part to refrain from introducing modern questions, or modern theological or philosophical categories in the organization of the material. Thus there is no one chapter on righteousness by faith, or ethics, or the ordination of women. Before one can use the insights of the apostle to answer modern questions one must understand the apostle in his own terms. As an effort in this direction I have chosen the apostle's own vocabulary and his concerns as guides.

Most of what is said here has been learned from the work that others have done. This is not an original piece of research. Rather, it is an attempt to put together a cohesive view of what seems to have been at the center of Paul's ministry. Much scholarly debate still goes on about many questions in Paul's letters. The positions taken here represent a judgment after serious study of the options and of the arguments for each. In matters of historical and theological scholarship there are no "assured results."

Achieving this cohesive view is complicated by the fact that the apostle did not write a comprehensive statement of his view of the Gospel. All his writings were prompted by the urgency of circumstances. Some are heatedly polemical; most of them are somewhat apologetic; all of them are true letters, lacking the stylistic polish expected from more self-concious efforts and having come about by the demands of urgent events. This means that it is difficult to assess what concerns really were at the center of the apostle's life. What is very important in a letter need not necessarily have been the overarching concern of the apostle's career, but only a live issue in one of the local congregations for a few months. It is well known that the apostle wrote more letters than those now found in the New Testament canon. Would our presentation of the apostle be significantly altered if we only had just one more letter of his?

It is the better part of wisdom to admit our limitations and to lay open our point of departure. Since we have what we have, there are many questions we cannot answer. On the basis of what we have, I have come to the conclusion that the best way to understand Paul is to recognize in him a man spurred on his mission by the realization of the imminent appearing of the Son of Man in glory. In other words, Paul's was an apocalyptic vision of the world and of human life in it.

Having laid out the task at hand and the point of departure, let me briefly explain the organization of this work. It consists of two sections. The first two chapters present a brief review of what, with historical confidence, can be said concerning the life of the apostle Paul. Here I need to put out a warning signal. Whereas the Pauline letters have some autobiographical information, and the Acts of the Apostles also provides some information about his life, both Paul and Luke had their own agendas. Therefore, at times, the only two sources at our command do not quite match. Impasses of this sort impose the need to exercise the historian's judgment.

Chapters 3 to 8 introduce the reader to Paul's main line of thought. In order to do this, it would seem most appropriate to follow one of two options: Either one could give a short introduction to each one of the Pauline letters in chronological order, or organize his thought according to the traditional theological rubrics: theology, Christology, anthropology, soteriology, eschatology, morality. Both of these plans of action, however, suffer from serious drawbacks. The first would be so bound to the historical circumstances and the issues of each letter that it would not allow for the comprehensive view I set out to achieve. The second forces the apostle into a way of doing theology which he knew nothing about since he was not the product of a European university.

I have opted for a compromise. I have singled out the letter to the Romans for special consideration since it is the one letter where the apostle did take time to discuss with some care the dynamics of God's dealings with humanity. Next I have singled out major theological words in the apostle's vocabulary in order to embody his thought in a way which, I trust, he would have recognized. These theological words have been paired in order to reflect the apostle's own dynamic integration and complementation of separate elements that bring to his thought both a frightful daring and a basic balance. I shall be rewarded if challenged by this approach my readers feel stimulated to pursue further after Paul's unique vision of things by more intensive study of the letters themselves with the aid of erudite commentaries.

As much as possible I have tried to stay away from modern controversies concerning points of interpretation in the Pauline corpus. This book is for the non-specialist who seeks a better understanding of Paul. I have not engaged myself in dialogue with my colleagues. Instead, I have stated as plainly as I could what I think to be the case, with minimal recourse to footnotes. Except for a few, most of them tell the reader where to find further discussion on the subject at hand.

In conclusion, I would like to thank those who have helped me in the completion of this project. First of all, I wish to acknowledge the stimulation of my many students, who imposed on me the necessity to come to a comprehensive view of Paul because otherwise I could not have been their teacher. Future students, I am sure, will still force me to re-evaluate things. A few colleagues read parts of the manuscript and offered helpful suggestions. I own much to Sister Maria Assunta Werner, CSC, my colleague at Saint Mary's College, for her careful reading and her many suggestions on matters of style. I would also like to single out Professor Earle Hilgert of McCormick Theological Seminary for his valuable criticisms. Linda Guyton and Linda Harrington typed early drafts as well as the one that went into the word processor. Their assistance and good cheer with this work is much appreciated. Finally, I would like to thank Dr. Robert Firth and Mrs. Pat Saliba of the Andrews University Press, for their efforts to make this project see daylight in print.

Herold Weiss

CHAPTER I

PAUL THE MAN

Seventy years after their deportation to Babylon, most Jews had established themselves in Babylonian society, and some had become prosperous in commerce, banking and government service. The stories of Daniel and Esther testify to their place in high society, and archaeological discoveries at Nippur tell the story of the smashing economic success of the local Jewish banking firm of Marashu's Sons. Even if their spiritual eyes looked toward Jerusalem, their feet were firmly settled in the fabric of everyday life in their new home. Cyrus' decree in 536 B.C.E. put an end to their exile and made it possible for them freely to go back and reclaim whatever property their ancestors may have had in Palestine. But most of them did not take advantage of the opportunity or had no property to reclaim. After having tasted the advantages of life in Babylon, at the center of world affairs where empires were won and lost, to live in the desolate Palestinian countryside must have seemed rather unattractive. There can be little doubt, even if exact figures are not available, that the Jews of the Diaspora far outnumbered those in Palestine.

Under the Persians the Jews fanned out from Babylon in all directions. Sometimes they were taken elsewhere on account of a specific plan for colonization by the government, but most often they went wherever their own interests took them, both West and East of Babylon. When Europe and Asia were for the first time truly opened to each other, after Alexander the Great's campaigns, the Jews enjoyed extensive rights of incorporation and special privileges under the law.[1] They could organize their communities within large cities both politically and religiously. At times these privileges even included exemption from military service since Jews would not serve on the Sabbath.[2]

According to rough estimates (the only kind possible on

1

account of the nature of our sources), at the time of Augustus Caesar there were about four and one-half million Jews in the Roman Empire, out of a total population of roughly fifty-five million. Cities like Alexandria, Damascus, and Antioch may have had close to a million Jews each. The Jews in Palestine were certainly a minority if one takes into account that Jews had settled all along the shores of the Mediterranean, in North Africa, Asia Minor, and Europe. East of the Euphrates, in the Parthian Empire, the Jewish population may have been even larger. The list of foreigners present at Jerusalem for Pentecost (Acts 2:9-11) around the year 32 C.E. mentions people from both sides of the Euphrates.

The religion of the Torah was prospering in the synagogues that little by little, nobody knows exactly how, began to be established wherever a few Jews had settled. The fact that large numbers of Jews were found throughout the Roman Empire may have been due, in some degree, to the missionary activities of the synagogues. A proper assessment of the number of proselytes within the synagogues is not easy to determine, however, and may have been exaggerated. To begin with, the synagogues were religious and community centers for Jews living far away from their homeland. In them the singing of psalms, the reading of the scriptures, and prayer took the place of attendance at the temple services.

Even though the life of Jews in the Diaspora was centered at the synagogue, that did not mean that the Jews lived in ghettos.[3] Many of them became outstanding leaders in their local communities and they took pains to make their religion known to their Gentile neighbors. Thus some Gentiles may have been attracted to the synagogues. The main appeals of Judaism to the Gentile onlooker were its monotheism and its high moral standard of conduct. Judaism also had antiquity to its credit, and antiquity lends authority.

THE CICILIAN CRADLE

Paul was born to a Jewish family which had maintained strong ties to its Hebrew past and had done well socially and economically in Tarsus. As the capital of the Roman province of Cilicia, Tarsus was "no mean city" (Acts 21:39). Besides its propitious location, with the Mediterranean in front, the Taurus Mountains behind, and the main road connecting Asia to Syria right through it, the city could boast of being one of the main centers of learning at the time. Probably only Athens and Alexandria outranked it academically. Strabo, the geographer, sometimes talks about it as if it were on a par with Athens.[4]

Throughout his life Paul felt good about his ancestry and his home town. Both gave him a sense of identity, and both made him proud. Trade and government had made Tarsus a flourishing Hellenistic city. For Paul, almost certainly, the city's attractiveness was found not so much in its active market place, but in the intellectual atmosphere fostered by Greek arts and letters. Unfortunately, with the sources we possess there is no way to determine whether or not he ever studied in Tarsus. We do not know how old he was when he went to Jerusalem. Did he go alone as a young man, after having received a basic education in Tarsus? Or did he go as a boy because his parents moved the family to Jerusalem?[5] He did feel some strong ties to Tarsus because when he received Christ's call to become an apostle for Him, after spending some time in Arabia and Damascus, Paul went to Tarsus and stayed there several years (Gal. 1:17, 21; Acts 11:25). To Arabia he went seeking the solitude of the desert. To Damascus he went seeking the fellowship of the first Christian community he had known. To Tarsus he seems to have gone seeking for his first mission field among those whom he knew from childhood. It would be interesting to know how the missionary apprentice was received by his home town. The autobiographical information he himself provides, however, is rather sketchy, and the Book of the Acts of the Apostles remains silent about those years of his life.

The authors of the New Testament did not write to satisfy our curiosity. Therefore, for some aspects of Paul's life we depend on our ability to read between the lines. It would seem reasonable to suppose that Paul received some kind of education at home in Tarsus before he set out for Jerusalem. There is no real evidence against this view. Even if his argumentative style is in the main Pharisaic, his writings show him knowledgeable of the ways of arguing developed by the Greek schools.[6] Still the evidence is inconclusive, and it may be fallacious to separate Judaic from Hellenistic ways of argumentation at a time when Judaism, even in Palestine, was thoroughly permeated by Hellenistic cultural influences. Yet one cannot help noticing the facts. After his short visit in Jerusalem with James three years after his encounter with

Christ on the Damascus Road, Paul himself remembers having gone
to Cilicia (Gal. 1:21). Apparently when searching for a place that
would welcome him, after Jerusalem proved to be less than friendly,
he thought of the familiar territory of his youth. Tarsus must
have been not just a place remembered from family lore but the
place where Paul spent his youth, and where he first discovered
the wide horizons of the world around him. Cilicia had been where
he had spun many dreams for his life. He felt good about being a
citizen of Tarsus.

Paul was also proud of his Jewish ancestry. Later in his
life, provoked by his opponents, he compared himself to them, and
found himself with a pedigree as good or maybe better than theirs:
"Are they Hebrews? So am I. Are they Israelites? So am I. Are
they descendants of Abraham? So am I" (II Cor. 11:22). Pondering
over the design God might have for the future of the Jewish
nation, Paul openly saw himself a part of it: "I also am an Israelite,
of the seed of Abraham, of the tribe of Benjamin" (Rom. 11:1).
And looking at himself in isolation, he saw in himself all the
marks distinguishing a man who, from a Jewish point of view,
could be happy with himself: "Circumcised on the eighth day, of
the people of Israel, of the tribe of Benjamin, a Hebrew born of
Hebrews, as to the law a Pharisee" (Phil. 3:5). These descriptions
make use of those terms that not only establish Paul's racial Jewish
descent but more specifically single out his religious position. The
archaic term "Hebrew" and the identification of the tribe of Benjamin point out that he was not a descendent of proselytes; neither
was he a descendent of some northern tribe that suffered deportation by the Assyrians and are commonly identified as the "lost
tribes." Judah and Benjamin were the two southern tribes that
composed the kingdom of the Davidic monarchy with its capital in
Jerusalem. As a descendent of Abraham, Paul was in principle a
member of the seed to whom the promises of the covenant had
been made. On account of his family and his race he stood in a
peculiar covenant relationship with God.

Paul's family must have been a member of the upper middle
class in Tarsus. As already mentioned, Jews enjoyed a favorable
legal status during most times, and many took advantage of this
and became citizens of their cities. The members of Paul's family
were citizens of Tarsus (Acts 21:39). More importantly, they were
Roman citizens as well (Acts 16:37). This was an honor which only

official Rome could grant and which Paul's family had obtained before his birth (Acts 22:28). Paul's ability as a tent-maker (Acts 18:3) should not be understood to indicate that his family belonged to Tarsus' lower working class. A close examination of his attitude toward manual labor reveals that working for a living was not something he inherited from his family. It was rather something he was willing to do as part of his commitment to work for Christ, even if it meant abandoning his former social standing.[7] The family's Roman citizenship reflects a high social position and, probably, was granted to it for having done some worthwhile service to the Empire.

JUDAISM IN THE DIASPORA

Diaspora Judaism always considered Jerusalem to be the focal point in God's plan for the world. The prophetic vision, best expressed in the second chapter of Isaiah, remained a living image in the minds and hearts of Jews everywhere. The prophet had said:

> And it shall come to pass in the last days that the mountain of the Lord's house shall be established in the top of the mountains, and shall be exalted above the hills; and all nations shall flow unto it. And many people shall go and say, Come ye, and let us go up to the mountain of the Lord, to the house of the God of Jacob: and He will teach us of His ways, and we will walk in His paths; for out of Zion shall go forth the law, and the word of the Lord from Jerusalem. (Isaiah 2:2, 3)

To be in Jerusalem for Passover at least once in his own lifetime was considered the religious duty of every Jew, no matter where he lived. But, to a large degree, Diaspora Judaism was beginning to come to terms with a *modus vivendi* independent from the temple, the priesthood, and the sacrificial system. The synagogue had practically replaced the temple as the place for religious gatherings. The singing of psalms, prayer, and the study of the scriptures had replaced sacrifices as the means of communication with God, and the scribes were beginning to achieve new power in the community as the mediators between God and humankind. In the Diaspora, Judaism developed not only new ways in which to preserve and live out its religious traditions, it also developed new ways of thinking. The cultural marketplace opened up by the campaigns of Alexander the Great forced Judaism to participate in the religious-philosophical dialogue taking place between East and West. Judaism had been nurtured in the East and had been expressed within the framework of the Semitic mentality. Now it found itself, to a large degree, in the West, and the process of cultural translation became an invigorating experience for the ancestral faith. The efforts spent relocating within a different cultural environment could not but force Judaism to re-examine itself, and to expand the implications of its faith in Yahweh within the larger framework of Greek culture.

The best known example of the impact of Hellenism on Judaism is the Septuagint--the scriptures of the Diaspora synagogues. According to tradition the first copy was commissioned for the library of Alexandria founded by Ptolemy Philadelphus around 265 B.C.E.[8] Seventy scholars collaborated in the translation from Hebrew to Greek. Whether this was actually the way in which the work was done is doubtful, but there is no doubt as to the effect that the Greek version of the Torah, the Prophets, and the Writings had within Judaism. Greek became the language of preaching and worship at the synagogues.

The reshaping of Judaism by a Hellenistic mold gave Judaism new tools with which to work out theological problems. Languages do not provide just words. They also clearly outline the kind of thoughts that are possible. Dressing the Old Testament in Greek meant also becoming aware of the philosophical considerations the Greeks had tried to solve with the words now being used to translate Hebrew words lacking such philosophical, legal, or moral connotations. Something happens to the discussion of God's dealings with man when the word "treaty" becomes the word "testament," or the word "faithfulness" becomes "righteousness," and the word "teaching" becomes "law." In Greek the Old Testament acquired new terminology and new connotations. The translators also felt embarrassed by the philosophical naivete with which the Old Testament spoke of God. Thus the Septuagint translators carefully softened those descriptions of God in the Old Testament which would have appeared crude anthropomorphism to Hellenistic readers. God's transcendence now had to be maintained. It was with the Septuagint that Judaism carried on its missionary efforts in the Diaspora and with which Paul would accomplish his own missionary activity later on. It was the Bible used at the synagogues of the Diaspora and as such provided the language of faith for the Jewish communities of the Mediterranean basin.[9]

The other source of information for the nature of the Hellenistic synagogues of the Diaspora is Philo, the great Alexandrian Jew who left us a veritable encyclopedia of Hellenistic learning at the service of the Jewish faith in Yahweh. Philo was many things at once, but first and foremost he was a Diaspora Jew who wished to exegete the Old Testament in a new way. As the basis of his monumental efforts was the need to preserve the religious traditions of the fathers in a manner which was intelligible both to himself and to his contemporaries. His basic exegetical method, according to which the words of the Old Testament are understood to have both a literal and an allegorical meaning, is one which Paul and other authors of the New Testament also used (I Cor. 10:1-12; Gal. 4:22-31; Matthew 13:36-43). How much of what we read in Philo is the product of his own genius and how much is the product of the exegesis going on at the synagogues of the Diaspora Sabbath after Sabbath is, at the present moment, difficult to determine. Yet there can be no question that the synagogue, in its missionary and apologetic efforts, had a weakness for disguising the teaching of the Hebrew prophets as compatible with, and capable of being understood as, the work of venerable Greek thinkers. The allegorical exegetical method itself had been devised by Greeks who wished to keep Homer culturally relevant after the classical age. In the hands of Philo the method was put at the service of the Pentateuch.

What was said above in no way should be taken to mean that Judaism was selling its soul to Greek culture or that Paul was trained in classical letters to the extent that Philo evidently had been. Moreover, it should be quite clear that Paul was never tempted to accommodate the Gospel of Jesus Christ to the wisdom of the Greeks. But this should not blind us to the fact that through the preaching of the Diaspora synagogues, which he attended regularly both before and after his call to be an apostle for Christ, Paul heard a great deal of popular Greek philosophy and acquired some of the terminology that he later put at the service of his work for Christ. Clear examples are the words "reason," "nature," "conscience," "duty," as well as figures of speech like the one comparing the law to a *paidagogos* (custodian of children).[10] At the local synagogue Paul may have also learned the popular lists of virtues and vices used by moralists throughout the Roman empire.[11] He used these lists himself in his own letters later in life, but it is clear that he thought that in the practice of virtue Christians were empowered by the Spirit and not by the light of reason, as taught by the moralists and even Philo.

Prior to the fall of Jerusalem in 70 C.E., and to its reorganizational in the following years, Judaism was a rather tolerant religion, where differences of opinion in matters of theological speculation or in religious practices, were looked upon leniently, even if at times they were not quite welcomed by some. Pharisees, Sadducees, Essenes, Herodians, Zealots, Disciples of John the Baptist, Therapeutai, and many other kinds of Jews lived with each other as best they could. Tensions among the groups were inevitable, but generally a spirit of tolerance permeated the Jewish social fabric.[12] Gamaliel's speech before the council at the time when Peter and John stood for trial, clearly reflects this spirit of tolerance. "Ye men of Israel," he said, "take heed to yourselves what ye intend to do as touching these men--and now I say to you, refrain from these men, and let them alone: for if this counsel or this work be of men, it will come to naught. But if it be of God, ye cannot overthrow it" (Acts 5:35-39).

Tolerance was characteristic primarily among the Pharisees, but it was not unknown to Sadducees, Herodians, and others. Thus, for example, there was within Judaism no set standard for admission. Apparently in Palestine any Gentile who wished to become a Jew needed to be circumcised. In this manner he became a proselyte and eventually a full member of the Jewish people. In the wilds of the Judean desert, however, the Essenes had their own set of standards to be met by anyone wishing to become an Essene. In the Diaspora, the synagogues were happy to have in their midst Gentiles who were not circumcised. Tolerance towards them was essential to attract them to the faith. Some apparently came to worship at the synagogue because they enjoyed the service. It was of a high intellectual and moral quality. These Gentiles were "God-worshippers." Others not only came to Sabbath services but also demonstrated their belief in God by living according to basic Jewish ways in terms of Sabbath observance, dietary laws, etc. These were "God-fearers." But since they were not circumcised, they remained Gentiles rather than proselytes. Whether or not it was possible really "to fear" God while being a Gentile was an open question within Judaism at the time. Undoubtedly some Jews thought it impossible. According to them if one really feared God, he would submit to circumcision and become a proselyte. The issue seems to have been much debated in the Hellenistic synagogues known by Paul.

PAUL AND PHARISAISM

As said above, it is not known under what circumstances Paul went to Jerusalem. What is known is that in Jerusalem he became a Pharisee and that he set for himself the goal to make a career within the movement (Phil. 3:5; Gal. l:14; Acts. 22:3). The picture of Pharisaism given in the Gospels reflects the high degree of tension that developed between Christianity and Pharisaism after the fall of Jerusalem. The meaning of the word in English common usage, where it is synonymous to *hypocrite*, does little justice to the rather broad, tolerant Pharisaism that existed prior to 70 C.E. The Pharisaism that attracted Paul was one that distinguished itself by its universalism, its apocalyptic view of the world, and its high regard for humans as God's special creatures. It was precisely the great value given to human beings, and their ability to understand and apply God's law to their lives, what gave Pharisaism its tolerance and its missionary outlook. The Pharisees were, after all, within the multifaceted Judaism of the first century, the clear descendants of the prophets. They spoke for God and taught the people what God's will was for them in terms of the real life situations facing them every day.

Over against the Sadducees who were conservative and literalists concerning the Torah, the Pharisees were content to let the Torah inform their everyday activities. Literalism allowed the Sadducees to ignore everything that was irrelevant to the lifestyle of a Jerusalem invaded by Hellenistic culture. Literalism also allowed the Sadducees to restrict Torah to the Mosaic canon. The teaching of the prophets could be safely ignored when it cut too close to the nerves of the priestly and landed aristocracy that constituted the core of the Saddusaic party. As long as things did not threaten the *status quo* the Sadducees were willing to let them slide. In the meantime, as men of affairs, they kept a firm grip on worldly matters and fully enjoyed their privileged status and prosperity.

By contrast, the Essenes denied that life in Jerusalem, and especially the cultic celebrations at the temple under Saddusaic control, was at all capable of being reconciled to the traditions of Judaism. Driven by a firm belief that the Day of the Lord was at hand, they retired to the Judean desert to keep themselves ceremonially pure and to prepare themselves for the ultimate battle between the cosmic forces of Good and Evil. In an effort to keep apace with the rhythm of Mediterranean commercial operations the Jerusalem establishment had adopted the Hellenistic calendar, but the Essenes, in defiance, celebrated the feast days according to the ancient Hebrew calendar and kept a different rhythm designed to alternate hours of work in the field with hours of prayer and hours for the study of the Scriptures. Their study was from the original Hebrew manuscripts, sometimes even retaining the already long abandoned ancient script. Central to the Essene community in the Judean desert was the work of its founder, known to us only as the Teacher of Righteousness, who also provided the community with the key for the interpretation of the scriptures and played a major role in the production of the commentaries on the books of the Old Testament found among the Dead Sea Scrolls.

Paul chose to become a Pharisee. In reference to the Sadducees and the Essenes, the Pharisees represented a mediating position. They were apocalyptically oriented but not obsessed like the Essenes. They lived in society in the midst of all its trials and temptations, but they were not thirsty for worldly power like the Sadducees. Unlike the Sadducees, who believed God left men alone to their own devices, and unlike the Essenes, who believed that human history is completely controlled by the divine will, the Pharisees believed that man's free will and God's providence operated side by side in some kind of undefinable tension. Therefore, even though the affairs of the world are ultimately in God's hands, human beings are responsible for their actions.

According to his own account (Gal 1:14), in his youth Paul proved himself a promising scholar. His later writings reveal that he profited well from his studies, since he was capable of doing typical rabbinic exegesis with assured confidence.[13] Exactly what goal he had set for himself within Pharisaism is not for us to determine with the sources at our command. There is no question, however, that when he embraced Pharisaism he did so along the more conservative lines upheld in Jerusalem, rather than along the more lenient lines allowed by the Diaspora. This is clearly revealed by his attitude toward the law while living as a Jew. In the application of the law to his daily living, with a clear conscience he could claim to have been "blameless" (Phil. 3:6). And as such he must have made an impression on his peers and his elders.

THE PERSECUTOR OF CHRISTIANS

The eager upstart within the Pharisaic party first came into contact with Christianity when he became a persecutor of this new group within Judaism. The reasons for, and the means used in, the persecution of Christians in Judea around the year 33 C.E. are very difficult to determine with any degree of historical certainty. In recent years two explanations have been given, but neither one seems compelling. Many modern students think that what provoked the Jewish leaders against Christian preachers was the fact that they were presenting Christ as an alternative to the Mosaic law. The argument goes something like this: Hellenistic Christianity preached salvation without the law. This was anathema to the Jews. As a result they took Stephen's life and drove the Hellenists from Jerusalem. In the meantime the Hebraists stayed in Jerusalem unmolested. The Jews had nothing against Jesus *per se* but could not tolerate the Christian claim that He replaced the law as the expression of God's will.[14] Paul thus became a persecutor of Hellenistic Christianity, and, when he was converted, he joined that very form of Christianity which he had formerly persecuted, proving that the notion of "justification apart from the law" (Rom 3:21) was not original with him but part of the Christian beliefs he received from his fellow Christian Hellenists at conversion. Later, when the Hellenists opened a mission to the Gentiles in which observance of the law was not taught, the Hebraists became opponents of the Hellenist Gentile mission. Then, as the main protagonist of the Gentile mission carried out by Christian Hellenists, Paul became a special target of Hebraist Christian persecutions. To the Hebraists the temple cult was central, and in the cult the distinction between Jews and Gentiles was firmly established. According to this argument, Jews, and Paul as one of them, persecuted only Hellenist Christians, like Stephen, because they were against the law and the temple. The other modern explanation of the case says that what provoked the Jewish persecution against the Christians was not their attitude toward the law, but their preaching that Jesus, a despicable Galilean, was the Messiah.[15]

Neither Paul himself nor the author of Acts tell us why he persecuted "the church of God." It would seem that to the first century Christian readers, who had probably experienced some form of persecution themselves at one time or another, the reason was well known. Modern attempts at an explanations have found clues either in Paul's own psychological make-up, or in an element of the Christian Gospel that excited the animosity of the rest of the Jews. Since it is clear that Paul was not the only one engaging in this activity, it seems perverse to credit Paul with deep psychological problems in order to account for his having persecuted Christians.[16] The reason, therefore, must be found in what, from the Jewish point of view, was problematic in Christianity.

Years later, when Paul wrote his letters, he could clearly distinguish his life as a Christian from his "former life in Judaism" (Gal. 1:13). However, even if he later saw Christianity and Judaism as two different periods in his own life, it must have been quite possible for him earlier to identify the followers of Christ as fellow Jews. It had been only logical for the Sanhedrin to consider that it had jurisdiction over them. Beating, flogging, and imprisonment were tools that it could legally use to discipline them. What caused Paul to engage in persecutions seems not to have been the perception of Christianity as a rival movement, offering an easier way of salvation, but as a movement within Judaism that needed some correction. It was not at all the case that the Jews considered Christianity to be a movement breaking away from Judaism and setting up an alternative to the law. What Christians were offering was an alternative interpretation of the law.

Several students of Paul have pointed out that there was nothing particularly threatening or capable of inciting animosity in a movement that proclaimed one of their own to be the Messiah.[17] Jewish messianism was flourishing at the time. But the very notion of Messiah was a fluid one, so that there were at least two or three different kinds of Messiahs expected by Jews of the time. It is, therefore, quite apparent that belief in Jesus as Messiah would not have been sufficient cause to persecute those who held such a belief.

If neither the claiming of messiahship for Jesus nor the

preaching of salvation apart from law may serve as legitimate explanations for the persecution of Christians on the part of Jews, the reason why Paul became a persecutor is to be found elsewhere. The clues are to be sought in what we know about messianic movements of the time and in what Paul himself considered to be the very core of Christianity.

Messianic movements in Judaism centered around individuals who were active and alive. It is true that Judas' movement (Acts 5:35-38), according to Josephus, survived and flowered into the zealot movement after the death of its founder. There is no question, however, that both he and his followers interpreted messiahship in strictly political and military terms. How specific Jesus' messiahship had been while he was alive is not easy to determine. It is undeniable, however, that in the eyes of his followers Jesus had acquired a messianic role before his crucifixion.[18] The Gospels make clear that the crucifixion of Jesus at first meant the collapse of the messianic hopes of his followers, and these hopes would have been crushed forever had it not been for Easter. Research into the Christological developments within the early church has shown that Messiah was not one of the early titles assigned to the Crucified and Risen One.[19] For all we know, the Jewish establishment, interested as it was in preserving the *status quo*, may have been particularly eager in having messianic pretenders crucified precisely because their hanging on a tree placed them under the divine curse promulgated by the law.[20]

It would seem, therefore, that within Judaism the Christian movement represented an anomaly in that serious claims about Jesus as messiah were made on his behalf by his followers in an intensified way only after his crucifixion, on account of his resurrection. Thus in the case of the Jesus movement, the crucifixion, instead of bringing to an end the messianic career of Jesus (as the Jewish leaders may have logically expected), only served to raise to a higher level the nature of the claims made on his behalf by his followers. From the Jewish perspective the obvious argument against these messianic claims was the undeniable fact of the cross. His having hung publicly exposed on a cross clearly disqualified him for any divine mission. He had died under God's curse.

As one who had "walked formerly in Judaism," Paul knew well that the word of the cross was a "stumbling block" to the Jews. From the Jewish perspective for anyone to make claims on behalf of a crucified man as a divine agent of any kind was obvious nonsense. But not only that, it was an open disregard for the specific teaching of the law on the one hand, while on the other appealing to the law in order to demonstrate that by this act divine promises had found fulfillment.

At the core of Paul's gospel is not the doctrine of salvation apart from the law but the significance of the cross of Jesus. Was his cross what disqualified him, or was his cross the demonstration of God's righteousness? The Christian tradition behind Paul was grounded on the death of Christ, on his cross (Phil. 2:8; I Cor. 15:3). For him the words of institution at the supper included the phrase "For as often as you eat this bread and drink the cup you proclaim the Lord's death until he comes," (I Cor. 11:26). As a Christian he directly linked persecutions and the cross. If he was being persecuted, he complained, it was precisely because he had not removed the stumbling block of the cross (Gal. 5:11). Moreover Paul charged those Christians who removed the stumbling block of the cross, and preached "circumcision" instead, to have done that in order to avoid being persecuted (Gal. 6:13). As far as Paul is concerned his opponents in Galatia were making the cross of Christ irrelevant (Gal. 2:21). At the core of the tradition received by Paul, and at the core of Paul's own gospel, no doubt, stood the cross of Christ. The question of salvation apart from the law was not primary but a corollary of the role assigned to the cross.[21]

The cross of Christ had certainly been a problem for the early Christians.[22] The followers of Jesus did not understand it when it took place, and many never recovered from its impact on their lives. For some of the disciples, however, in the light of the resurrection the cross became the very act of God that brings about freedom from death. Thus if it is true that Paul converted to the very form of Christianity which he had formerly persecuted, it is clear that he had persecuted Jews who preached the Crucified One as the manifestation of God's righteousness.

To the Jewish authorities it must have been incomprehensible, and therefore reprehensible, that Jews should take upon themselves the task of making such claims for one who, according to the law, was a reprobate in the sight of God. All forms of Judaism in existence were based on defensible appeals to the law. In this Christians were no different. Yet their claims were in explicit contradiction to the law.

In his persecuting activities against Christians, Paul was not a member of a mob reacting on the basis of emotions to what some individual Christian may have said in an unguarded moment. Rather he was a thoughtful person ready to argue against "the gospel" being preached by some Jews. His was part of a concerted effort under the auspices of the High Priest to bring Christianity to account for its teachings. Paul's activities as a persecutor were sanctioned by the very right the Jews had within the Empire to take care of internal matters in their own courts, according to their own laws. If the kind of treatment Paul later received from his Jewish brethren when he went to preach Christ in their synagogues is any indication of what Jews could do to discipline their own, it is clear that when Paul was himself engaged in "persecuting the church" he must have been instrumental in administering floggings and the famous forty lashes minus one to those in Judaea who believed in the cursed Crucified One. Apparently in this activity, he was extremely zealous, thus surpassing his fellow young upstarts in his concern to uphold the traditions of the fathers (Gal. 1:13, 14).

Even if the disciplinary measures administered within the confines of the synagogues and the local Sanhedrins could be quite harsh, it is not necessary to suppose that Paul's persecuting activities sought the death of his victims.[23] It was expected that the administration of discipline would induce the disciples of the Crucified One to desist from making claims of cosmic import for the cross of Jesus of Nazareth. Arguments and discipline should have been enough to prove their views to be contrary to the Torah. It was on account of his success in the Judean countryside that Paul was sent with letters of introduction and instructions to Damascus, the largest city in the region south of Antioch where a large Jewish community had settled in the Diaspora and where apparently Christians were increasing their numbers with ease.

CHAPTER II

PAUL THE APOSTLE

The Book of the Acts of the Apostles pictures Paul as a Jew who kept strong ties with Judaism throughout his life. Scholars have tended to discount this theme in Acts as part and parcel of Luke's efforts to find in Judaism the ancient tradition that gives Christianity legitimacy and authority.[1] Yet Paul's own letters have nothing that contradicts the general picture of Paul in this respect. On the contrary, as said in the previous chapter, Paul understood his own life in terms of two periods, a Jewish and a Christian one. As a Christian he no longer saw the Jew as superior to the Gentile. Rather he saw redeemed humanity as one in which all standard ways of dividing it no longer held. Still he continued to consider Judaism as an indispensable heritage and often repeated the refrain "to the Jew first, and also to the Greek."

The only thing about his Jewish past Paul ever regretted was having been a persecutor of Christians (I Cor. 15:9). By instinct throughout his life he identified himself with Jews. Almost always when in his letters he says "we" he means "we Jews." There is no indication that after having been confronted by Christ on the Damascus road he wished to cease being a Jew. Of his life as a Jew prior to the Damascus experience, he could conscientiously declare that it had been blameless (Phil. 3:6). Considering the Christian community at large, he saw himself, Peter, and indeed the majority, as "Jews by nature" (Gal. 2:15). His Jewish heritage was for him an argument that helped to prove that God had not given up on the Jews (Rom. 11:1-3).

16

PAUL'S CONVERSION

The experience of Paul on the road to Damascus did, undoubtedly, make a radical difference in his life. But did this experience create a radical discontinuity between his past and his future?[2] Did Paul go through a "conversion experience"? It must be recognized that between the Paul before Damascus and the Paul after Damascus there is more continuity than discontinuity. It may not even be said that on the road to Damascus he found a new religion, even if undoubtedly he found a new Lord. He does refer to the early part of his life as his "former life in Judaism" (Gal. 1:13), but that by itself does not make clear specifically what is now "former" in his life. Certainly throughout his life he always worshipped the same God who made the promise to Abraham. Near the gates to Damascus he did not change religions, rather he changed his mission. Whereas before he had been engaged on a mission on behalf of the Sanhedrin, he now became engaged on a mission on behalf of the Crucified One who lived. He received a call to a new ministry. That is why the language Paul uses to describe his encounter with Jesus Christ echoes the call to a prophetic ministry in the cases of Jeremiah, Isaiah, and Ezekiel.[3]

Admittedly the relationship between Paul the Jew and Paul the Christian was a bit ambiguous. Still there are some elements in this transition which are fairly clear. It would seem that as a Christian Paul would have seen nothing wrong if another Christian of Jewish origin would as a Christian continue to "live like a Jew," but he would stand firm against a fellow Christian who would contend that living "like a Jew" was of the essence in Christianity. In the Epistle to the Galatians he made quite clear that "the truth of the Gospel" has taken away the significance of "living like a Jew." Therefore, Paul was not at all timid in charging Peter with distorting the Gospel (Gal. 2:11-14).

It must be made clear, however, that Paul's eagerness to establish the relative value of living like a Jew, once one had become a Christian, was not motivated by his frustrations with Judaism. As far as we can tell, while a Jew Paul had been happy and secure in his way of life. He did not come to Christ in order to be delivered from a life of spiritual breakdowns full of unhappy memories. He had not been a guilt-ridden Jew.[4] He was not trying to escape the accusing finger of the law (I Cor. 4:4). Only later,

when Christians had found a way of accounting for themselves as
Christians and of viewing their historical connections to Judaism
from a new perspective, they saw the Jewish way of life in the
law as burdensome. At that time the wounds left by the trauma of
the break from Judaism were still very painful, and under these
circumstances Christianity, unfortunately, became anti-Jewish. The
apostle Paul, however, did not see things that way. Paul did not
speak of the Jewish way of life as a "burden" or as "a yoke upon
the neck . . . which neither our fathers nor we have been able to
bear" (Acts 15:28, 10). The yoke referred to in Peter's speech was
considered oppressive, so that Christians were glad not to have to
bear it. But Paul himself found nothing intrinsically wrong with
life in Judaism. Paul thought that, given the alternatives available
prior to Christ's Cross, those who were Jews and lived like Jews
had every advantage indeed (Rom. 3:1-4a).

It should not surprise us, therefore, to see that Paul is
concerned to define who is the "real Jew" (Rom. 2:28, 29) or who
are the "true sons" of Abraham (Gal. 3:29, II Cor. 11:22). Paul
never disentangled himself from Judaism *per se* as an element in
his past he would rather forget. As a matter of fact, having met
Christ did not make him deny that he was a Jew, a Hebrew, a
Benjaminite, and a Pharisee. Before having met Christ he may
have boasted about these things. Now after having met Christ he
would have Christ's example in mind. Christ, being equal with God,
had not given significance to what he was in order to become a
man, a servant, and die on a cross. Paul would also scorn whatever
he may have been, and count it all as lost in order to imitate
Christ (Phil. 3:8).

What, then, was the Damascus road experience all about?
The Acts of the Apostles contains three versions of what happened,
and in his letters Paul makes a tangential reference to that part
of his life while defending the divine origin of his apostolic authority. Paul's own words are found in Galatians 1:15f., "But when he
who had set me apart before I was born, and had called me through
his grace, was pleased to reveal his Son to me, in order that I
might preach him among the Gentiles, I did not confer with flesh
and blood." Paul's words clearly reflect the words of the prophets
when describing their call to the prophetic office. The language
clearly sets out his new mission to the Gentiles. As Paul saw it
years after, when the Son was revealed to him, he did not change

his religion; he changed his mission and his understanding of the divine timetable. The one who had been persecuting the church under the authority of the chief priests now became the one preaching the Son to the Gentiles under the authority of God himself. Looking back to that experience on the Damascus road, Paul does not consider it to have been what made him a Christian and caused him to cease being a Jew. Rather, it provided him with his commission to be a preacher of Christ to the Gentiles. It would seem that for Paul having become a Christian and having become an apostle were one and the same thing. Becoming both of these, however, he did not cease being a Jew.

Undoubtedly Paul must have been baptized, but he never made reference to that experience in his writings even though it is quite clear that he understood baptism as of transcendental importance (Rom. 6:1-11).[5] The accounts of the Damascus experience in Acts mention his baptism (Acts 9:18; 22:16). From the evidence one gains the impression that the author of Acts was a more methodical writer than Paul. He organized things neatly with a view to telling the story clearly and in order (Luke 1:3). Thus in his account of the Damascus road experience we find Paul going through the classic steps. First, he receives the Holy Spirit, then he is baptized, finally he begins to preach; but as soon as he begins to preach there is a threat to his life. Thus he moves from Damascus to Jerusalem, to Caesarea, to Tarsus (Acts 9:17c-30). The same pattern from Damascus to the Gentiles by way of Jerusalem is found in the speeches of Paul before the Roman procurators at Caesarea (Acts 22:17-21; 26:30). All the evidence testifies to Paul's movement toward the Gentiles immediately after Damascus.

Most significant about the accounts in Acts is that when confronted by the risen Christ Paul does not ask, "What must I do to be saved?" The reported question is "Lord, what would you have me do?" (Acts 9:6; 22:10). And the answer given to Paul's question is not "Repent, and believe in the Gospel." Rather it is "The God of our Fathers has chosen you . . . and you shall be his witness unto all men of what you have seen and heard (Acts 22:1-4, 15) . . . and of those things in which I shall appear to you delivering you from the Gentiles unto whom I now send you" (Acts 26:16c, 17). The three accounts in Acts vary as to the exact words and as to whether the words were spoken by the Lord to Ananias (Acts 9:15), or by Ananias to Paul in Damascus (Acts 22:14, 15), or

by the Lord directly to Paul on the road (Acts 26:16, 17). As reported, the words reflect the concerns of Christians of a later
generation. Still one thing is clear, meeting Christ Paul did not just
become a Christian. He became one sent on a mission to the Gentiles. One may wonder whether Paul understood at the time what
his acceptance of Christ as Lord would do to his Judaism. It is
certain, however, that it put an end to his persecuting activities.
Under his newly-found Lord, he obviously continued worshipping
the same God.[6]

In order to understand the issue we are considering we may
with profit also notice the way in which the accounts in Acts
refer to Ananias, the one who gave Paul back his sight and baptized
him. According to Acts 9, Ananias was "a certain disciple." Here
Ananias is presented as a Christian who has heard of the evils Paul
has been performing against the churches in Judaea on account of
the authority given him by the chief priests to punish all those
who believe in Jesus (9:10, 13, 14). In Acts 22, however, Ananias is
described as "a devout man according to the law, well spoken by
all the Jews who lived there" (22:12). Clearly Ananias is here considered the perfect Jew, living like a Jew within the synagogue.
Yet this prototype of the good Jew is the one who baptizes Paul
into Christianity. Clearly this version of the story reflects no
distinction being made between disciples of Jesus and good Jews.

Recent studies in the Book of Acts have made it quite clear
that the author wrote it with a definite theological perspective
and with the clear intention to present the history of the early
church as that of the instrument of God that represents the logical
fulfillment and legitimate inheritor of the Old Testament promises.[7]
It is important for the author of Acts, therefore, to show the continuity that exists between truly devout Jews and Christians. On
the other hand, it is also important for him to present the unbelieving Jews as essentially trouble-makers and obdurate opponents
of the work of the Christian missionaries. Within this Lukan pattern,
Paul represents the pious Jew who having started as a persecutor
of Christianity, becomes a Christian missionary. To some this
presentation of Paul is in opposition to the picture of Paul that is
gained by reading his own letters. Thus Bornkamm has said, "To
the end of his life Luke's Paul continues to be an orthodox Jew
and Pharisee; for Christ's sake the real Paul gave up the Law as a
means of Salvation."[8] This statement is worthy of careful

consideration. It is meant to explain Paul's relationship to Judaism on the basis of a distinction between the real Paul who broke with Judaism and Luke's Paul who remains a good Jew in an idyllic Christian community that is at home with the Jews.

Undoubtedly, there are distinguishable differences between the Paul that one meets by reading his own letters and the Paul that is presented to us by Luke in the Book of Acts. Luke's Paul is a faithful participant in synagogue worship and is eager to celebrate Passover in Jerusalem. At the temple he joins reactionary Christian Jews in Nazarite vows in an attempt to show to one and all what a good Jew he really was. All this does not quite fit the picture of Paul the proclaimer of the Gospel that God's righteousness has now been demonstrated apart from the law (Rom. 3:21) and is not at all attainable by "works of law" (Gal. 2:16). If, as Paul says, "Christ, our paschal lamb, has been sacrificed" (I Cor. 5:7), there seems to be no reason for anyone to make a dangerous trip to Jerusalem in order to be there for Passover.   Still Bornkamm's statement offers a false alternative.

It is quite true that, as Bornkamm states, the real Paul gave up the law as a means of salvation. But does it follow from this that Paul no longer sees himself as an orthodox Jew? To speak of orthodox Judaism in the time of Paul is somewhat anachronistic. As was pointed out already in the previous chapter,[9] Judaism at the time of Paul was characterized by its fluidity--not by its orthodoxy. Judaism came to an "orthodoxy" only in the second century. Therefore, to distinguish the real Paul from orthodox Judaism is not quite possible.

When Luke's Paul is to be contrasted with the Paul of the epistles, one must also consider the way in which Paul evaluated his own previous experience as a Jew once he became a Christian. The primary text is Philippians 3. The chapter starts with a strident warning against evil workers, who are also called dogs (a rather common and derogatory way for Jews to call Gentiles, cf. Mk. 7:27). Then the apostle goes on to make a distinction between the evildoers who belong to the "incision" and "we" who belong to the "circumcision," it is clear that he is engaged in a polemic with some people at Philippi. Apparently these evildoers, among other evils, are considered by Paul to be apostles of the circumcision, which Paul here sarcastically calls "mutilation." By contrast, he says, "We are the circumcision, who worship God in the spirit and glory (boast) in Christ Jesus and find no confidence in the flesh" (3:3). The language is somewhat reminiscent of that found in Galatians 6:13. Even though the two passages contrast those "who desire to have you circumcised that they may glory (boast) in your flesh" (Gal. 6:13) with those who like Paul glory (boast) in Christ Jesus and put no confidence in the flesh" (Phil 3:3), the consistency in Paul's own position does not mean that his opponents in these two cities held similar views.

What is significant for our purpose is that Paul has found a word, incision, with which to characterize circumcision as a basis for confidence in the flesh in order to be able to characterize himself as part of the circumcision. Obviously, at Philippi the word *circumcision* had not become the slogan it had been at Galatia. The false apostles confusing the Galatians had been using the word circumcision as the catchword with which to insist that Christians were supposed to "live like Jews." As we have already seen,[10] this much Paul explicitly denied. At Philippi the word had not been the catchword used to distinguish friend from foe. Thus in his epistle to the Philippians Paul uses the word to describe his Christian view of things. It would seem, therefore, that Paul was able to distinguish between "boasting in the flesh," or confidence in the law as a means of justification, or of perfecting those already in Christ, and being a Jew. Giving up one did not necessarily mean giving up the other. In practice, he realized that as long as he lived "in the flesh" he would remain a Jew. The alternative would have been to become a Gentile, but that was no alternative since it would have been giving significance to distinctions which "in Christ" had become meaningless. Therefore, he worshipped God "in the spirit," but the externals of his worship were Jewish. This means that the picture given by Luke of a Paul who throughout his life remains a pious Jew and a Pharisee who, "as his custom was," naturally attended the local synagogue on the Sabbath, if properly balanced by the primary evidence given by Paul in his own letters, may be taken seriously.

We shall proceed then, recognizing that Paul always felt himself a kinsman of the Jews and could speak of them as "my brethren" (Rom. 9:3). This means that the confrontation with Christ on the Damascus road was more in the nature of a prophetic call than a traumatic uprooting from His Jewish past. He was baptized, that is true. But his baptism was a way of becoming one with

Christ in the power of his death and resurrection. It was what had effectively transferred him to a life under the rule of Christ.

PAUL AND JERUSALEM

The Book of Acts conceives the missionary activity of the church as taking place according to a pattern. Witnesses are to go out from Jerusalem to Judea to Samaria and to the ends of the earth (Acts 1:8). Therefore, it is not surprising that all three accounts of Paul's call at Damascus bring him to Jerusalem shortly after his baptism (Acts 9:26; 22:17; 26:20). But there their agreement ends. Therefore, the details of Paul's experiences in Jerusalem, as presented in Acts, are difficult to establish. According to Acts 26, Paul came to Jerusalem and preached Christ to the Jews, then he moved on to Judea, and then to the Gentiles (26:20). In Acts 22 we are told that Paul came to the temple in a despondent mood because the Christians in Jerusalem were avoiding him on account of his former role as an official persecutor of Christians. It was while praying at the temple that he received a vision commissioning him to leave the Jerusalem community and go to the Gentiles (22:21). Acts 9, however, presents us with a still different account. There we read that when Paul was met with a cold shoulder by the leaders of the church in Jerusalem, Barnabas arranged for an introduction that opened the way for Paul to join the community and made it possible for him to stay in the city and preach. Thus, it was only when he met with the enmity of Diaspora Jews that Paul left Jerusalem, with the protection and the blessing of the Jerusalem leaders. Against these three accounts, with all their own differences in details, stands Paul's own testimony. He claims not to have gone to Jerusalem at all (Gal. 1:17). Instead, he went to Arabia and after three years met with Peter for fifteen days in Jerusalem (Gal. 1:18).

In the overall plan for his two volume work, Luke has assigned to Jerusalem a most significant role.[11] It serves as the institutional base for what is best in Judaism and also as the home base for Christianity. Luke concentrates the appearances of the Risen Christ in Jerusalem and makes the Council of Jerusalem responsible for solving the issue of the role of the Jewish laws in a Christian's life. Paul, however, knows nothing about the Jerusalem

Council's decision on this matter and seems to plan his activity so as to keep himself independent from Jerusalem. In this he follows the pattern of the Old Testament prophets who also remained independent from the centers of religious and/or political power.[12] This is not to deny Paul's explicit identification with the tradition of Jesus that had come to him directly, and to which the Jerusalem disciples were also legitimate witness (I Cor. 11:23; 15:2). He did not become an agent of official Christianity as he had been an agent of official Judaism. His Damascus experience did not mean replacing the official letters of the High Priest with official letters of the leaders of the Christian movement at Jerusalem. Damascus was not primarily the exchange of Judaism for Christianity. More significantly, it meant for Paul the abandonment of his role as an agent for human authorities in order to become an apostle of the Risen Christ. Not even Luke's explicit efforts to tie Paul to Jerusalem could quite blur the ambiguities that characterized Paul's relationships with the Jerusalem Christian authorities.[13] The different traditions about the nature and the circumstances of Paul's first visit to Jerusalem after the Damascus experience point out the tensions that existed between Paul and Jerusalem Christianity.

In his autobiographical outline Paul is primarily motivated by his desire to establish his independence from the Jerusalem leaders, whom he does not take too seriously (Gal. 2:6).[14] His apparent disdain for the pillars of the Jerusalem church should, however, be understood in context. It must be remembered that Paul did not take himself too seriously either. His personal relations with the Jerusalem Christians "who were of repute" (Gal. 2:2, 6) were not governed by his own feelings of superiority *vis à vis* them. If he had compared himself to them from a human point of view, probably he would have found himself just as good as they. But there is good evidence to show that he recognized them as legitimate overseers of the Christian movement. The point is that the Jerusalem leaders had no authority in themselves. It is when these leaders are compared with Christ himself as a source of authority that the vacuity of any personal claims to authority by the Jerusalem leaders becomes apparent. On the basis of the divine authority that was communicated to him by revelation, Paul carried on his apostleship on a parallel course to that travelled by the Jerusalem leaders. With the Jerusalem leaders he would coordinate his own missionary effort; but he would never work for them or submit to their demands. He had only one Lord: Christ himself.

Paul's commission as an apostle, as far as he himself was concerned, did not have its origin on the authority of any man, not even the pillars of the Jerusalem community. His commission had been given directly to him by Jesus Christ himself. Human intermediaries would not have established his apostleship more firmly. They would only have made it derivative, second-hand. Throughout his ministry Paul apparently met the opposition of those who questioned his claim to be an apostle. He was not one of the twelve disciples who received their commissioning from Jesus. Neither had he received his commissioning from the leaders at Jerusalem. Lacking this kind of authorization, Paul was left open to the charge of being a false apostle. By contrast, other missionaries could present to the members of Paul's churches letters signed by the Jerusalem leaders that confirmed their authorization to preach (II Cor. 3:1f.). Paul, however, defends his apostleship as being of divine origin and certified by the work of the Holy Spirit in his ministry (II Cor. 3:3f.; 10:8). When he compares himself to the "superlative apostles" making the rounds in his churches in order to challenge his apostolic authority, he finds himself "not in the least inferior" (I Cor. 11:5). To his own question "Are they servants of Christ?" he himself gives the answer, "I am a better one" (I Cor. 11:23a). Paul indefatigably defended both the validity of his mission and his independence from the Jerusalem leaders on account of the fact that the Spirit had confirmed his ministry by the presence of new Christian churches. Letters of authorization signed by the Jerusalem leaders could add nothing to the legitimacy of his apostleship, even if other apostles were abroad claiming better connections as guarantees for their mission.[15]

Paul's account of the incident that took place at the table fellowship of the Christian community in Antioch (Gal. 2:11-14) also reveals that he did not consider the Jerusalem apostles as his superiors. In order to know exactly what transpired in Antioch we would have to have Peter's version of the incident. Paul's version, however, makes quite clear that Paul did not think much of James, as the one who sent investigators to Antioch, nor of Peter and his double standards. The tone of Paul's remarks speaks louder than any actual words.

Also revealing of Paul's attitude toward Jerusalem is the way in which he elaborates allegorically on the notion that to claim sonship from Abraham is not enough since, after all, Abraham had two sons, and only one of them became an heir. Thus more significant than to establish who is one's father is to establish who is one's mother. Paul appeals to the story in Genesis in order to reject Jerusalem and the preachers of circumcisions that have come from it (Gal. 4:25, 30). He brings to mind the stories of Sarah and Hagar (Gen. 21:1-14), and their respective sons, in order to explicate the significance of the contemporary situation in Galatia. According to Paul, when the story is considered an allegory Hagar represents "the Jerusalem that now is," which is to be distinguished from "the Jerusalem above" represented by Sarah. Thus just as in the story of Genesis Hagar and her son made life difficult for Sarah's son, so also it now happens that "the Jerusalem that now is" and her missionaries make life difficult for the children of the Jerusalem that is above. Since the story says that eventually Hagar and her son were cast out of the household, so also now "the Jerusalem that now is" and her sons should be cast out from the Galatian churches.[16]

The fact that Paul chose to charter a path for himself where his loyalty to the Risen Lord exceeded his loyalty to Jerusalem should not be interpreted to mean that he was at odds with the mother church. As A. D. Nock has said, "Unlimited deference could be shown to the older disciples as a matter of charity, but no obedience could be yielded to them as a matter of authority."[17] This does not deny that between the apostle to the Gentiles and the Jerusalem community there were fundamental agreements. Both Paul's theology and Paul's missionary activities were intimately tied to the Christian community which, prior to 70 C.E., certainly had its center in Jerusalem.

Immediately after the death and resurrection of Jesus the early Christian community in Jerusalem began to seek ways to explain how it was possible for the one who had been crucified to be actually the agent of God's salvation. The resurrection certainly opened up for the disciples a whole new panorama within which to find the significance of the life of the one who had been crucified and thereby had died under a curse. It was in a renewed study of the Old Testament Scriptures that the role of the cross in Jesus' life came to be accounted for. This was certainly done prior to Paul's becoming a Christian. In fact it had provoked Paul's persecuting activities against the Church.

Paul did not produce a new theology of the cross over against the theology of Jerusalem. He certainly accepted the proclamation of the Gospel that he knew from his days as a persecutor. He not only integrated himself within the stream of witness to the resurrection (I Cor. 15:8), but he also thought out with radical consistency the implications of Jesus' cross as God's saving act for mankind. Even if the consistency with which Paul drove the original premises to their logical conclusions left some fellow Christians wondering whether they could follow Paul all the way, Paul blazed a theological trail by himself, or at least with little company. He felt secure that the Lord to whom he had committed his life was with him. As a faithful servant of his Master, however, he found himself at times in rather awkward positions *vis à vis* the leadership of the movement to which he belonged.

THE JERUSALEM COUNCIL

One of the most puzzling episodes in the whole history of Paul's relationship with the Jerusalem church is his participation in what has come to be called the Jerusalem Council (49-50 C.E.), which issued the Apostolic Decree quoted in Acts 15:23-29. Historical scholarship has never been able to arrive at a very satisfactory reconstruction of the events that led to, and actually transpired at, that meeting of Christian leaders at Jerusalem. Several questions remain unanswerable. If Gal. 2:1-11 is also an account of this meeting, this would be Paul's second trip to Jerusalem. According to Acts this would be his third or fourth trip (Acts 9:28; 11:27-30; 12:25; 15:1-3). Was the meeting called by the Jerusalem leaders, or by the Antiochene community, or by Paul himself, acting under revelation? What was the outcome of the meeting? Are Acts 15 and Gal. 2 referring to the same meeting? Answers to these questions are difficult to arrive at. Still no matter how one accounts for the differences between Acts 15 and Gal. 2, and whether or not one thinks that Acts 15 and Gal. 2 refer to the same event, it is clear that Paul's theology and Paul's activity were not informed by the Apostolic Decree of Acts 15. On account of reasons unknown to us, Paul never makes reference to the Apostolic Decree in his letters, even though he could have done so to advantage on several occasions. Therefore, the events narrated in Acts 15 do not help us to establish the nature of Paul's relationship with Jerusalem.[18]

In Galatians 2, Paul reveals his understanding of the agreement he had reached with the pillars of the Church in Jerusalem. After he revealed to them the gospel he was preaching among the Gentiles (for already seventeen years!), he specifically declares "those who were of repute added nothing to me" (2:6). Instead it was agreed that Paul should go (together with Barnabas) to the Gentiles, and that James, Peter and John should go to the Jews. In other words, the pillars of the church in Jerusalem were not to interfere with the mission of Paul among the Gentiles, just as Paul was not interfering with things among the Jews.[19] In this way, and by resisting efforts made by some to have Titus circumcised, Paul is happy to report that "the truth of the Gospel" was preserved for the Gentiles (2:5). It is quite clear that Paul came to Jerusalem not because he was called in for questioning, but rather he came of his own accord in order to have the interference from missionaries sent from Jerusalem stopped. These people had come to the churches he had founded and had insisted that to be Christians the Gentiles had first to become Jews. To them Christianity was a Jewish sect, just like the Pharisees or the Essenes. Together with some others, Paul insisted that Christianity was a kind of Judaism that was unique in that it was meant for mankind without asking whether people were Jews or Gentiles. If a circumcised person accepted Christ's lordship that was fine. But if he did it uncircumcised, it was too late to circumcise him now. After the resurrection of Christ the barriers that have commonly been used to make distinctions among humans had become irrelevant. "There is neither Jew nor Greek, there is neither slave nor free, there is neither male nor female, for you are all one in Christ Jesus" (Gal. 3:28).

THE COLLECTION

It would appear from Paul's letters that the Jerusalem leaders proved themselves unable to stop the continuation of missionary activity among Paul's converts by some who claimed to have the support of the Jerusalem church leaders. Whether these missionaries actually did have such backing is another matter. There is no reason to doubt that, just as Paul, the leaders at Jerusalem also lived by the agreement sealed between them by "the right hand of fellowship" (Gal. 2:9).[20] Paul's letters do confirm, moreover, that Paul did live up to his agreement with the Jerusalem community on another matter: helping the Jerusalem poor. It is quite clear that "The Collection" represented for Paul the concrete means by which he kept his ties to Jerusalem.

The problem of the Jerusalem Christians was aggravated precisely because they lived among the Jews in order to carry on a mission to the Jews. They were conscious of the importance of a Christian witness in Jerusalem, but this left them at a marked financial disadvantage because they were experiencing the contempt of the community at large and the disapproval of their immediate families (Mk. 3:31-35, Mt. 12:46-50, Lk, 8:19-21, Mk. 13:12-13, Mt. 10:21, 22, Lk. 21:16, Mk. 10:29-30, Mt. 19:29, Lk. 18:29, 30, Lk.14:26). This must have left Christian converts, particularly in Jerusalem, without economic means of support. Since Paul agreed that these Christians should remain in Jerusalem and carry on a Christian mission to the circumcision, he promised to provide economic help for the poor in Jerusalem. Since there is ample evidence in his letters to indicate that "the collection" was a major preoccupation of his ministry, it is difficult to account for the fact that it plays no role in Luke's account.

Paul's relations with the Jerusalem Christian community was epitomized by "the collection."[21] At the meeting described in Gal. 2, one of the possible outcomes certainly was a division of Christianity between its Jewish and its Gentile branches. But "the freedom that Christians have in Christ Jesus" (2:4) prevailed and thus the agreement already mentioned was arrived at. Instead of two Christianities there was to be one Christianity with two missions. What Paul emphasized was the unity. He took pains to explain that the two missions--one to the uncircumcised and one to the circumcised--were activated or promoted by one and the same Power (2:8). The visible and tangible expression of the unity of the two missions was the contribution made by the Gentiles to support the economic hardships of the Jewish Christians in Jerusalem. In this way "the collection" was a constant reminder that the churches of the Gentiles were not isolated, independent, or ungrateful beneficiaries of the events that had taken place in Jerusalem.

Paul's relation to Jerusalem was ambivalent. For the authorization of his mission he was independent, but he wanted his mission tied to the mission of the circumcision based in Jerusalem. It is somewhat ironic, therefore, that it was because of his identification with "the collection" and of his desire to take it to Jerusalem personally that he relented in his desire to go to Rome and went to Jerusalem instead, only to be made a prisoner at the temple. Probably those who instigated the riot that brought about his arrest were actually Jewish Christians who still did not agree to the accord privately worked out between Paul and the pillars of the Jerusalem Christian community (Gal. 2:2). Acts blames "Jews from Asia" (21:27) for Paul's arrest, but they must have been members of the Christian synagogues who were annoyed by Paul's activities within the Christian community. Writing after Christianity had broken away from Judaism, about 90 C.E., Luke no longer remembers the struggles that had plagued the life of the early church. Paul's troubles in Jerusalem in the Spring of 58 C.E., however, may not have been totally due to the animosity of Jews who had nothing to do with Christianity. His antagonists, we may safely surmise, were Jewish Christians.

THE MISSION TO THE GENTILES

There is no doubt that Paul's career as an apostle in the prophetic tradition did not endear him either to the majority of the members, or the leaders, of the struggling new movement which had not yet become quite aware of its own relationships with its Jewish roots. Both the Epistle of James and the Second Epistle of Peter testify to the fact that, not long after his death, misunderstandings of Paul's preaching were abroad in the land. Later, in the second century, by twisting his words the Gnostics found in him their mentor.[22] But already throughout his lifetime, apparently, it was not uncommon for him to be misunderstood. Part of the problem may have been the fact that his work was for the Gentiles, but somehow it was built around the synagogues that had attracted the Gentiles to the God of Abraham, Isaac, and Jacob in the first place. This missionary tactic left him open to misunderstandings. Was he trying to build the synagogue on a new basis, or was he trying to destroy the synagogue? If Acts serves as our guide, at every town where there was a synagogue, Paul began his mission there. How could he claim, therefore, to be an apostle to the uncircumcision when he was always working among the circumcised in the Diaspora? Was he just going to the synagogue in order to reach the God-worshippers and the God-fearers who could be found there? From his own letters it is quite evident that his preaching presupposed a knowledge of the Old Testament on the part of his audience. As Paul saw it (Rom. 3:21, 31), Christ could not be understood apart from the Old Testament and faith in Christ is a requirement established by it. It is also clear that some of his converts were susceptible to being swayed by other Christian missionaries to be circumcised, and thus became Jews in order to be able to be Christians. This means that they could understand the claims the Old Testament made on Christianity.

These difficulties only emphasize the lack of a clear-cut way of differentiating between Judaism and Christianity during the years of Paul's missionary activities. Paul did become a central figure in this transition process because he was among the first ones to see clearly that Christianity was something so radically new that it could not be contained within Judaism. The inner working power of the new wine had burst the old wine-skins.[23]

Paul's entanglements with the Jews and the Jewish Christians should not prevent us from taking notice of his clear sense of responsibility toward mankind. There is no doubt that he addressed Gentiles directly. The "truth of the Gospel" knew no boundaries made by nature, political realities, or religious laws. In the Gospel there is neither male nor female, neither Greek nor Barbarian, neither Jew nor Gentile. As he said, "I am under obligation both to Greeks and to barbarians, both to the wise and to the foolish" (Rom. 1:14). It cannot be supposed, therefore, that Paul preached the Gospel only to people who were already under the umbrella of the synagogue and could make sense of his anchoring of the Gospel within the framework of Israel's understanding of God's work in history. Whether or not Acts 17 reports Paul's actual words in the Areopagus, there is no reason to doubt that Paul actually preached in Athens with some success, both in the synagogue and the market place. The names of Paul's converts in Athens were well known even a generation later when the Book of Acts was written, and among them was Dionysius the Areopagite (Acts 17:34). Paul himself reports that he was rather pleased of his work among the Gentiles, not that he had done it himself, but that he had been used by

Jesus Christ to bring about the obedience of faith among the
Gentiles (Rom. 15:17, 18).

Paul's missionary activities in the eastern half of the Mediterranean cannot be traced with much precision from his own letters.
The Book of Acts has neatly systematized Paul's travels into three
missionary journeys and the final trip to Rome as a prisoner seeking
justice from Nero. But these narratives are also rather sketchy at
best. We would like to know more about Paul the founder and
pastor of churches throughout Asia Minor, Greece, Macedonia, and
Dalmatia. From Acts one learns only of two extended periods of
pastoral activity: a year and a half at Corinth (Acts 18:11) during
the second journey, and two years and three months at Ephesus
(Acts 19:8, 10) during the third. Ephesus seems to have served as
a center of operations for other parts of Asia Minor (Acts 19:10)
and even for some pastoral trips across the Aegean to Corinth for
fence-mending (II Cor. 2:1). Antioch on the Orontes in Syria served
as operational base for Cyprus and southeast Asia Minor. Ephesus
gave him access to central and western Asia Minor. Philippi, a
church with which he had a specially warm relationship, may have
sponsored his efforts in Macedonia, Greece, and the eastern Adriatic
coast.   On the well-kept Roman road network it was relatively
easy from these cities to fan out to the nearby towns. Paul's
activity seems to have concentrated in these urban centers. Paul's
own letters make quite clear that a few years after Jesus' death,
Christianity had ceased being a movement addressed to peasants in
the parabolic language of the countryside. Paul's Christianity is an
urban movement skipping from city to city. Instead of making
reference to sowers and their seeds, fishermen and their nets,
treasure buried in fields, and absentee landlords, Paul's metaphors
bring out what preoccupies the urban masses: the law courts, the
theatre, and sports.

Even though it is not unusual to think of Paul as the lone
traveler along the excellent Roman highways, his missionary activity
never was a private affair. He worked as the member of a team in
which he seems not to have made much of his position of leadership.
He involved others in his work and fully shared himself with them.
Among his associates, Sosthenes, Silvanus and Timothy are named
as co-authors of some of his letters (1 Cor. 1:1; 2 Cor. 1:1; 1
Thess. 1:1; Phil. 1:1), and he credits Silvanus and Timothy with
having shared in the preaching of the Gospel at Corinth (2 Cor.

1:19). At the time of the Corinthian correspondence, Titus, his "partner and fellow-worker" (2 Cor. 8:6, 23; 12:18), was Paul's intermediary (2 Cor. 2:13; 8:16) while Apollo, whom Paul had urged to visit Corinth, preferred to stay away while the situation in Corinth remained unpleasant (1 Cor. 16:12). Of all his fellow-workers he had the most intimate sentiments for Timothy. He wrote of him, "I have no one like him, who will be genuinely anxious for your welfare. They all look after their own interests, not those of Jesus Christ. But Timothy's worth you know, how as a son with a father he has served with me in the gospel" (Phil. 2:20-22). Others designated as fellow-workers are Urbanus (Rom. 16:9), Philemon (Philemon 1), Mark, Aristarchus, Demas, Luke (Philemon 24), and Epaphras, who is called a fellow-prisoner (Philemon 23). Special mention is to be made of the wife-husband team of Priscilla and Aquila, also called fellow-workers (Rom. 16:3; 1 Cor. 16:19), and Andronicus and Junias, a Jewish couple who were "notable among the apostles" (Rom. 16:7). Both in Ephesus and in Rome the home of Prisca and Aquila had become a Christian meeting house (1 Cor. 16:19; Rom. 16:5). We also know of the churches that met at the home of Philemon (Philemon 2), Gaius (Rom. 16:23) and Nimpha (Col. 4:15). Within the larger Pauline circle of servants of Christ "working hard" for the Lord, Paul mentions Mary and Persis (Rom. 16:6, 12), and Tryphaena and Tryphosa (Rom. 16:12), apparently a working team of two sisters. From this evidence it would appear that the Christian missionaries with whom Paul shared his own ministry were fully integrated and that they discriminated neither against Jews or Gentiles nor against women. Anyone could become a full apostolic partner in the work of the Gospel.[24]

Paul's great dream as an apostle was to preach the Gospel of Jesus Christ at the western frontier of the Roman world. Spain seems to have held a special allurement to his mind. Spain had been developing as a major center of commerce and culture for some centuries already. Some prominent Roman families had branches in Spain. One of Paul's most famous contemporaries, the philosopher Seneca, was a Spaniard. His was a patrician family that had settled in Cordoba years before. Several members of the family attained prominence: Lucan, the poet of the *Pharsalia*, was Seneca's nephew, and Gallio, the proconsul of Achaia before whom Paul was accused by the Jews in Corinth (Acts 18:12), was Seneca's brother. Other Spaniards attained even higher rank and became emperors. Traffic between Rome and Spain was heavy. Reading the Roman authors who were contemporaries of Paul one gets the impression that the Romans saw the East as the source of strange customs and religions, Germany as a frontier to be defended, and France (Gaul) as a place to which one could be banished. Spain, on the other hand, was a Roman land where Roman culture was beginning to flourish. This was especially true along the valleys of the Ebro and the Guadalquivir. For the Roman no place on earth was anywhere close to being capable of comparison with Rome, yet Spain had an idyllic charm of her own. The fact that there was nothing farther west may have contributed to this sentiment about Spain. It was also Rome's first province taken from Carthage at the time of the Punic Wars.

Paul was also under the spell of Spain (Rom. 15:24, 28). Tradition has it that he fulfilled this urge after his first hearing before Nero.[25] The Book of Acts leaves him in Rome preaching freely. In this way the author of Acts completes his own vision of the advance of the Gospel from Galilee to Jerusalem and from Jerusalem to Rome. But our own curiosity about Paul's last years is left unsatisfied. Did he ever go to Spain? There is no way of knowing with the evidence now available.

Any attempt to date specific events in Paul's life encounters major obstacles. Still it is possible, with some degree of certainty, to give approximate dates to some of these.[26] It seems that it was in the spring of 58 C.E. that, at the midpoint of his third missionary journey, Paul was back in Corinth. Before arriving he had been actively engaged in gathering the collection for the poor at Jerusalem. He had written letters to the Corinthians about the significance of the collection and the need for them to be putting aside money for this purpose before his arrival.[27] Apparently when he arrived at Corinth he found himself in possession of enough money to make it imperative that the money be taken to Jerusalem. Paul had come to Corinth expecting to continue west to Rome and then to Spain. Now the collection stood in the way. It had to be taken to Jerusalem.

The decision he made that spring at Corinth proved to be one of the most significant of his entire life. Rome had a special meaning to a citizen of the empire. Paul knew that a well-established Christian community already existed there. He had met some of the members of that community in his travels in other parts of the empire. It may very well be that in his view of things he could see that eventually Rome had to be the center of a Christianity that was addressed to mankind without reference to barriers imposed artificially, like the one separating Jew from Gentile. Apparently from Corinth Paul looked at Rome as the operational base for his future missionary efforts in the West (Rom 15:28). Antioch, Ephesus, and Corinth had served him well as bases for operations in the eastern half of the Mediterranean basin. But the coast of Dalmatia was more or less the limit of what could be reached easily from Corinth. Having completed the preaching of the Gospel to the east of the Adriatic, he now wished to cross that sea and go west to Italy and Spain (Rom. 15:19). Spain seems to have been what pulled him westward. He had no particular interest to work where others had worked before (Rom. 15:20). Pulling him East was the obligation to take the collection to those who needed it. The need of the poor in Jerusalem was real and had to be taken care of. His concern over their precarious situation at the center of the Jewish focus of power and influence was only matched by his concern to abide by his promise to the Jerusalem leaders. The collection, as was said before, also was for Paul the tangible way of tying together the Christian communities from Jerusalem to Illyricum, what today is western Yugoslavia, before he ever embarked on further ventures to the West.

Thus it was that in the spring of 58 Paul left Corinth for Jerusalem rather than for Rome. His dream to be an apostle for Christ in Spain may have been shattered that day, even though Paul did not realize it at the time. He must have felt that the interests of the churches he had already founded were more important than those of the churches he may have been able to found in the future and that the needs of the poor in Jerusalem were more urgent than his personal desire to go to Spain. The labors of twenty years were not to be imperiled by a personal urge to go to new frontiers in the West. The unity of the church in the East had first to be cemented by delivering the collection in Jerusalem. Spain could wait (Rom. 15:28-29).

What makes Paul's decision to go to Jerusalem all the more admirable is that at Corinth, while making his decision, he was perfectly aware that at Jerusalem he was to face opposition both from unbelievers and from the saints (Rom 15:31). That unbelievers who had admired him as a persecutor of Christians would be unhappy with him as an apostle of Christ is quite understandable. That the saints would find his service for Jerusalem unacceptable makes us pause to reflect again about Paul's relationship with Jerusalem. It is certainly extraordinary for him to say that he has been doing "service for Jerusalem." The phrase sets apart the things God had done through him in Christ in his ministry among the Gentiles (Rom. 15:16-19) from the things he has been trying to do in order to fulfill his obligation to the leaders of the Jerusalem Church.

Paul feels quite different about these two things. Of his work among the Gentiles, which he carried out *in* Christ and *before* God, he is quite confident (Rom.15:17). His efforts to collect money for the saints among the churches in Macedonia and Achaia (Rom 15:26) are a different matter. He is happy that the members of these churches were pleased to contribute (Rom. 15:26, 27), but he is not sure that the Saints in Jerusalem will accept his own efforts on their behalf. This service for Jerusalem is characterized, however, by its temporal character. He hopes to complete it soon (Rom. 15:28) and then to be free to go on with his mission to Spain. By contrast his work for God is something from which he never could free himself.

We can only speculate as to the motives for Paul's urge to go to Spain. In no way need we doubt the sincerity of his desire to go there to preach the gospel among those who had not yet heard it. He was legitimately looking for new fields of labor. According to him he had finished his work from Jerusalem to Illyricum, but neither Acts nor his own letters tell us anything about any missionary activity in Illyricum. It was an extraordinary feat to have done so much in just a few years, if indeed the Gospel of Christ "had been completed" in these territories. In most human affairs there is more than one factor influencing human actions. It would not be in any way detracting from Paul, or his integrity, to suggest that perhaps his desire to go to Spain imme-diately after having finished his "service for Jerusalem" may have been somewhat influenced by his desire to find fields of labor where the influence of Jerusalem would be less strong. He must have been growing tired of continuous battles with opponents who claimed a Jerusalem connection.

CAESAR'S PRISONER

The account of Paul's arrival in Jerusalem that we have in Acts is quite problematic. On the one hand, we learn that Paul and his companions had a happy meeting with James and all the elders (Acts 21:17-19). After the initial joyous acceptance of the reports of Paul's missionary success (and, presumably, of the collection about which Acts says nothing),[28] Paul is warned that Jewish Christians are upset with his preaching of Christian freedom. The fear of the Christian elders is based on what fellow Christians who are zealous for the law may do to Paul. So these leaders urge Paul to join a group of Jewish Christians in a Nazarite rite.

Some have suggested that the only reason Paul agreed to participate in the Nazarite vows was that it would facilitate the acceptance of the collection by the Jerusalem community.[29] This is not necessary, however, since it can be argued that the logic of his teaching is not against his participation in a Nazarite rite. Expressions of piety to the God of Abraham, who is the Father of Jesus Christ, could certainly follow Jewish custom. As a logical corollary, there would be nothing wrong for Gentile Christians to express their piety to the God of Abraham along non-Jewish traditions that were not morally reprehensible, if while doing so they were not compromising their participation in the death of Jesus on the cross. Luke correctly reports that the rumor that Paul had been teaching Jews not "to live like Jews" (Acts 21:21) is false. Paul was against Jews demanding that Gentiles "live like Jews" (Gal. 2:10-14). In this way they were placing a premium on "circumcision." But piety needs to be expressed and there was nothing wrong in expressing it in a traditional manner. In principle he could become a Jew to the Jews in order to save the Jews (1 Cor. 9:20). Luke's narrative of the activities of Paul in Jerusalem are patently marked with Luke's concern to show Jews and Gentiles being reconciled in the person of Paul. Paul's trip to Jerusalem with the collection, as reported in Romans, was undertaken precisely with that same purpose in view.

On account of the Nazarite vows in which he agreed to participate, Paul found himself repeatedly at the temple. On one such occasion a mob stormed him and accused him of having brought a Gentile into the court of the men. That the accusation was false is made clear by everything we know about Paul. He may have brought Titus to Jerusalem as a test case in order to force an issue within the Christian community (Gal. 2:1, 3-5) but he knew better than to challenge Judaism at the temple by bringing a Gentile into the court of Israel. Each one of the nine doors connecting the court of the Gentiles to the court of the women or the court of the men had a sign clearly stating that any Gentile entering beyond that door would be held responsible for his own death.[30]

The exact nature of what transpired at Jerusalem is beyond historical reconstruction. Paul himself speaks of going to Jerusalem in order to deliver the collection which he had been taking among the churches of Macedonia and Greece for the benefit of the Jerusalem poor (Rom. 15:25, 26). Acts, on the other hand, reports that he cut his hair on account of a vow, wishing to be in Jerusalem for Passover (18:18, 21) and completely ignores the existence of a collection for the poor. Since we have only partial accounts, it is difficult to specify the circumstances that brought Paul back to Jerusalem. In spite of this fact, it is not difficult to understand how Paul could have became a prisoner of the Roman procurators at Caesarea-on-the-Sea in those troubled years that preceded the Jewish War of 66-73 C.E.

In the hands of the Romans Paul was safe on account of his Roman citizenship. Roman citizenship or not, the Roman procurators were not going to miss the opportunity to use Paul for their own purposes in the rather explosive political climate prevalent in Palestine at that time. It did not take Paul long to realize the futility of any hope that his case would be judged on its own merits. He was going to be used to appease either the Jews or the Gentiles, whichever appeared to need appeasement according to the whims of the Procurator. The Romans, it is easy to understand, could not quite make sense of a Jew who claimed to be a real Jew while the Jews in the gallery shouted against him. Hoping to get some insight into this difficult case, the Roman Procurator sought the advice of Agrippa II, a great-grandson of Herod the Great. Agrippa was half-Jewish, but like his father, grandfather, and great-grandfather before him, he had been educated in Rome and counted among his friends members of Rome's imperial families. At the time, Agrippa was ruling territories between Palestine and Syria for the Romans. As a respected and prominent member of the Herodian dynasty, he may have been expected to give some good advice as to how best to use Paul in terms of the tense situation that made governing Palestine a difficult job. Frustrated by his inability to get a decision even though his innocence was clear, Paul appealed to Caesar. The political climate in Palestine precluded a fair trial. In the midst of the tensions that eventually erupted and brought about the destruction of the Temple, Paul, taking advantage of his Roman citizenship, asked that his case be tried before Caesar.

According to Luke, Paul's trip to Rome did not take place as one of Paul's missionary journeys but as a prisoner seeking justice at a higher court. As noted above, two years earlier, when at Corinth, Paul had wanted to go to Rome and from there to new fields of labor in Spain, but out of a sense of duty he had gone to Jerusalem with the collection. We know about this from his letter to the Romans, but the author of The Acts of the Apostles apparently does not know about Paul's letters. It is doubtful, therefore, that he knew about Paul's plans to work in Spain or of his desire to establish some sort of a base camp in Rome for his future work in the western Mediterranean. Paul's own letters from prison, Philemon and Philippians, do not specify from which prison they were written.[31] Their geographical provenance is, therefore, uncertain even if later they were said to have been sent from Rome. In Acts Paul's trip to Rome as a prisoner is described in some detail, including some magical demonstrations of power (Acts 28:3-6). Luke's narrative of the trip to Rome, however, is not related to Paul's expressed wish to visit Rome (Rom.15:28). Rather it is integral to Luke's own vision of the expansion of Christianity from Jerusalem to Judaea, Samaria, and the ends of the earth (Acts 1:8).

The trip to Rome proved to be most eventful, and the author of Acts, using the travel diary of one of Paul's companions, gives a rather detailed account of the journey. It started on a merchant ship as far as Myra in Lycia. There the Roman centurion taking Paul to Rome decided to change ships and arranged for the continuation of the trip on a larger ship that made the run from Alexandria to Rome. By now the shipping season was over and the winds were unpredictable. Still, against Paul's advice, the shipmaster and the owner insisted on going on. First they were detained by lack of winds, but later a great storm broke loose as they were making the crossing between Crete and Malta. For a while it seemed that all was lost. In an effort to save their lives, first the cargo and then some of the ship's rigging were thrown overboard. For days they drifted, tossed by the sea. Eventually, they suffered shipwreck on Malta, where they spent the winter. Finally, Paul and his companions reached Puteoli, in the Bay of Naples, in the spring of 61 C.E. A journey which under normal circumstances would have taken 8 days had taken six months. From Puteoli they walked to Rome on the Via Appia.

The Book of the Acts of the Apostles closes with Paul safe in Rome. Luke says that he rented an apartment and preached the gospel with liberty (Acts 28:30-31). It is clear that Luke chose to end his account there because his intention was to show how the Roman authorities had consistently not only allowed, but even encouraged, the preaching of the Kingdom of God within the Empire. For reasons of his own, again, Luke does not satisfy our curiosity about important events in Paul's last years. What was the outcome of his trial? Did he regain his freedom to travel or was he paroled in Rome? Did he satisfy his desire to go to Spain? What were the circumstances of his death? Luke must have known the answer to each one of these questions, but he chose not to tell.[32]

Other admirers of Paul in the last decade of the first century and later believed he had gone to Spain and that he had eventually suffered martyrdom during the reign of Nero, which would mean that he died before 68 C.E. Clement of Rome makes the second point quite explicit and strongly suggests the first in his letter to the Corinthians (5:4-7). Around the year 200 C.E., Caius of Rome testifies that on the road to Ostia, after leaving the city, one comes to a monument marking the spot of Paul's burial.[33] Eventually a large basilica was built on this spot and a large statue of the apostle stands now in the atrium. Unlike the basilica of St. Peter in the Vatican, where extensive archaeological excavations have uncovered the monument that Caius says marked the place of Peter's burial, the basilica of St. Paul Outside the Walls has not been excavated. Paul's final resting place remains unmolested by the archaeologist's spade.

AN OVERVIEW

The extent of Paul's accomplishments as the Apostle to the Gentiles was never recognized during his life-time. His letters provide ample evidence of the extent and the nature of the opposition he had to face from fellow Christians who did not agree with his understanding of the significance of the death and the resurrection of Jesus Christ. Luke, writing 25 years after the apostle's death, presents the Jews as the source of the apostle's constant difficulties in Asia Minor, Corinth, Ephesus, and Jerusalem. Paul's own letters reflect a historical situation which Luke chose to forget. He looks back and sees an ideal early church totally united in love. Paul knew a Christian movement that was characterized by rather harsh battles and unpleasant circumstances. Among many other things, we know that at one point, under the influence of other "apostles," even one of the churches that he himself had founded embarrassed him and sent him off rebuked when he tried to mend the irregular situation that had developed in that church (II Cor. 2:1-3).

Paul's own catalogue of the many hardships that he had endured in the pursuit of his mission (II Cor. 11:21-33) includes a reference to five times having received the infamous thirty-nine lashes "at the hands of Jews" (11:24). It is not clear, however, whether those who applied to him the discipline of the synagogue were Jews whom Paul had tried to persuade of the Gospel of Jesus Christ or Jewish Christians who violently disagreed with the way in which Paul saw Jews and Gentiles standing on an equal footing before God once they were "in Christ." What is clear is that the life of the apostle took place in the midst of a great debate within Christianity as to its relationship to Judaism, its sister faith.

CHAPTER III

THE LETTER TO THE ROMANS

Among the letters of Paul, Romans stands out as somewhat different from the others in that it is almost impossible to determine the circumstances existing in the church at Rome which prompted him to write. All his other letters were written because Paul needed to address himself to a particular situation in a church. It would seem that Romans is different in that while in his other letters Paul is reacting to existing conditions in one of his churches, Paul wrote Romans in order to initiate a relationship with a church he had not founded himself. Many scholars have attempted to make Romans conform to the general pattern and have tried to deduce from the letter the situation in the church of Rome which prompted Paul to write. But the task has proven extremely difficult.[1]

According to Paul himself, the letter was written to let the Romans know that on account of his responsibility for the safe arrival of the collection to the proper hands at Jerusalem, his proposed trip to Rome was being postponed until further notice (15:23-28). The elaborate argument developed in the letter makes obvious, however, that informing the Romans about changes in his travel plans may not have been the main reason for writing the letter at all.

Even if the concrete historical circumstances under which the letter to the Romans was written are unknown to us, the central theme of the letter's argument suggests that there were at Rome certain tensions between Jews and Gentiles which Paul wished to help resolve. Thus the letter deals with how the Gospel of Jesus Christ affects both groups. What is not clear is how much the Roman Christian community had separated itself from the Synagogue. Thus what Paul has to say may have to do with Jews and Gentiles who were within the Synagogue and had come in contact with preaching about Jesus Christ, or it may have to do with a situation in an already distinctly Christian Synagogue. In the letter, Paul seems to be always aware of the objections, or the reactions, which Jews may have in reference to what he is writing.[2] Thus even though Paul's argument is addressed to both Jews and Gentiles, often special attention seems to be given to the Jews. Paul seems intent that they come to understand what it is all about.

And what is it that Romans is all about? This question is particularly appropriate for Romans. It would be harder to answer in reference to, for example, I Corinthians, which seems to be about a number of things. Romans is about how the Gospel affects both Jews and Gentiles. In short, one could say that the Gospel does the same thing for both. But within the religious-historical perspective of the Jews, the distinction between Jews and Gentiles was considered essential. No one could erase that distinction without a satisfactory explanation. In Romans Paul attempts to give precisely such an argument.

After the usual epistolary heading, with its benediction and thanksgiving, Paul opens his exposition by stating a thesis: The Gospel is the power of God for salvation . . . to the Jew first and also to the Greek (1:16). The apostle also explains that the Gospel, as the power of God for salvation, reveals God's righteousness (1:17), but God's righteousness is revealed within a world which also reveals God's wrath (1:18). This is the thesis. Basically it is a simple thesis, and Paul works out its basic argument in 1:18-4:25. To come to terms with it we can do no better than to follow closely Paul's own presentation.

THE WRATH OF GOD

Leaving aside for the moment his demonstration of how God's righteousness is revealed, in 1:18b-32 Paul presents a rather depressing picture of what individuals are capable of doing when they become the object of God's wrath and God withdraws from them. God may reveal himself to humanity in two contrasting ways. God, we may say, has two aspects, and Paul chooses to speak of the dark side of God first. God may open up to man as wrath.[3] The important thing for our purposes here is to understand that God's wrath may be seen quite readily right here on earth. God's wrath is not spoken of by Paul in reference to a description of God. To see God's wrath one does not look at God. Rather, one looks at men and women. When God in his wrath gives up humanity the consequences are immediately worked out. As Paul sees it, God's wrath is revealed by people who, knowing better, "suppress the truth" and exchange the glory of the immortal God for images "of created, mortal things" (1:18-23). As a result, in his wrath God gives up mankind to all kinds of distorted and unnatural acts of their own wicked devising. Three times in these verses Paul stresses that the wickedness of mankind is due to the fact that in his wrath God has given them up (1:24, 26, 28). In other words, when Paul views sinful mankind Paul sees God's face looking in a different direction. In this way, Paul recognizes that mankind's life in wickedness does not take place in a universe without God. Neither is it due to the promptings of an agent of evil, who can somehow bypass God's care for his creation. Why mankind "suppressed the truth" is not to be explained. Yet mankind's life as if there were no Creator reveals God's wrath in that, under this condition, it is almost inevitable that men and women can only sink lower and lower into a depraved existence. In this description of humanity under God's wrath, where idolatry and sexual immorality are presented as the main evidence, Paul exemplifies the basic tenets of Judaism.[4] Moreover, as a true worshipper of Jahweh, Paul cannot bring into service a second god as the god of evil. He is certainly a monotheist, and he recognizes that in a universe where there is only one God even evil must somehow be related to Him. The existence of evil men and women only serves to reveal the dark side of God.

For all practical purposes, at the end of chapter one Paul has drawn the backdrop for his picture of God's righteousness. He realizes, however, that what he has just said may be misunderstood, so he decides to clear the air of any possible misunderstanding before he moves ahead with his thesis.

What he had said in 1:18-32 could have lead Jews to understand the Pauline description of those under God's wrath as a reference to the Gentiles. After all, in the Jewish mind Gentile and sinner were synonymous terms, and Paul the Jew knew it very well (Gal. 2:15). Paul digresses, therefore, to make clear that those who reveal God's wrath are not only the Gentiles, but also the Jews. In the process Paul also advances the argument by making clear that these men and women he is talking about not only demonstrate

God's wrath, but are in fact sinners. Chapter two opens telling the Jews in the audience that God's wrath, or judgment as a negative sentence (2:3), also reaches them. As a matter of fact, the tribulation and distress brought about by God's sentence will fall upon "every human being who does evil, the Jew first and also the Gentile" (2:10). Paul is here talking to the Jews in his audience. This whole section is special for them, to prevent them from thinking that in 1:18-32 he was talking of Gentiles. Here he talks to the Jews in their terms, and makes clear that even though they have the law, the fact that they transgress the law only intensifies their predicament. Undoubtedly possession of the law makes a difference, but it gives only apparent grounds for boasting. The sarcastic tone of 2:17-20 is quite obvious.[5] If Paul grants the Jews a privileged position, it is only in order to establish their greater responsibility for their sin.

Verses 14-16 have been read to mean that Paul is saying that if the Jews would only live up to what the law requires, they would be saved. The same would be true of the Gentiles, who, even though they do not have knowledge of the law, do have a conscience that tells them what is right. If they would only live up to their conscience, they would be saved. Such a reading of the text is far removed from Paul's mind, as the immediate context and the whole of Paul's writings make clear. Paul is not saying that living up to one's available standard of good works would bring him or her salvation. Paul is only stating the fact that with the law or without the law people turn to doing something other than what their better judgment requires of them. If one were to see things as the Jews do, one would come out only agreeing that men and women are sinners. The Jews with the law are inexcusable sinners, and the Gentiles with their consciences are in the same category. The Gentiles may find at times their consciences more flexible than the Jewish law, so that they may actually use them to excuse themselves, but their consciences, in fact, accuse them. The whole section only seeks to establish that God's wrath is manifested in mankind's wickedness (3:9b).

Reading these verses one finds an easily detectable bit of sarcasm in Paul. He grants the Jew his pride in his religion (the law) and his pride in his race (circumcision), only to turn both upside down in comic caricature. Paul is obviously taking into account a possible Jewish reaction to 1:18-32, using Jewish ways of thinking to advance his own point of view. As he sees it, people are either under the power of God at work in the Gospel (1:16) or under the power of sin (3:9). Sinful Jews are, therefore, no different from sinful Gentiles. God's wrath is manifested in both, and as a result both sink deeper into sin. To drive his point home, Paul uses quotations from Scripture that declare the Jews to be sinners just as much as the Gentiles (3:10-18). The Psalms say it best, "No one does good, not even one" (14:1). The Pauline conclusion is "all have sinned and fall short of the glory of God" (3:23). No Jew would have argued against the notion that the Gentiles are sinners, but Paul wishes the Jews to see that they are too. Therefore, he argues on their terms. Here Paul has been working with a Jewish definition of sin. It is an act performed contrary to the law, or to the conscience. It is not clear that Paul on his own would have used this definition of sin. Later in this letter, when working out practical problems, he sees sin not against law, but against faith (14:23). Still sin and law are related, not as antagonists however, but as collaborators.

THE RIGHTEOUSNESS OF GOD

In order to follow Paul's argument it is important to determine the meaning that he gives to two key terms: faith and righteousness. These words carry different meanings for different authors. Therefore, it is absolutely necessary to make sure that Paul's meaning is understood. The very fact that Paul avoids the word justice, in Greek *dike*, and uses the word righteousness, *dikaiosyne*, instead shows that he was aware of the significance of these words. Apparently he used *dikaiosyne* in order to remain within the Old Testament, rather than in the Greco-Roman tradition. In the forensic tradition justice is an ideal represented by a blind-folded woman with a balance in one hand and a sword in the other. She stands for impartiality, equity, the ability to evaluate fairly and to punish responsibly. These qualities, however, are abstractions which make it possible to conceive a just society according to these ideal criteria. Within this framework, justice is something which must be present in the mind of the legislator and of the judge, so that they might create and maintain a just society.

In the Hebrew mind justice is essentially neither distributive nor punitive, nor vindicative according to abstract notions that exist in the minds of the leaders of society. Rather, justice is what all members of society do, or refuse to do, when they remain faithful to the way in which God ordained things when he created the world. The hellenization of Judaism led some Jews to think of the law as the formal manifestation of knowledge itself (2:20), which otherwise consistently resists encapsulation and remains an idea. Paul clearly does not see things this way. Following the most traditional Jewish way of seeing things, he does not consider the law as the concretization of knowledge, or wisdom, or justice. Rather, justice finds concrete expression in the every-day lives of human beings and God. Justice, then, is not a state in which those who are just find themselves, but an activity done in accordance with the purposes of God who above all else is the Creator. The Old Testament prophets do not admonish the people to acquire justice as if it were a desirable condition in which to live. They insist that all, especially the leaders of the people, must *do* justice in their daily activities. They think that for a people who knows itself as the object of God's electing love, through which God intends to fulfill his purposes with creation, to do justice should be natural. They are, therefore, amazed to discover that experience disproves their expectations.[6]

The authors of the Old Testament do not consider God an idea that imposes itself by logical necessity. He is a person that discloses itself to human beings through actions. Therefore, the actions of God are just because He determines His own activity as God. The law and justice are not conceived as independent entities capable of evaluating divine activity. Since within reality every thing, whether Creator or creature, has a specific purpose for its existence, things or beings are just when they fulfill the purpose of their existence. In other words, justice is done when the purposes of the Creator are fulfilled. To Jeremiah, the ease with which the birds of passage migrate should be matched by humans in their fulfillment of their divinely appointed purposes (8:7).

For the Hebrews, righteousness could only be conceived by observing actual manifestations of it in concrete action. Specifically, someone or something could be spoken of as just or righteous only when what had been intended at its creation has come to be demonstrated in actual performance. Balances are righteous when they measure weights accurately. People are righteous when their every-day lives fulfill the expectations of their Creator and Saviour.

But when is God righteous? Certainly, his righteousness is not established by a law external to Him. Is God judged by His law? Logical consistency would demand that God keep the commandments of His own law. The demonstration of consistency, however, drove some Rabbis into rather bizarre arguments.[7] In the Old Testament, God is not righteous because He is impartial and at his court all are equal before the law, thus guaranteeing equity to all. Rather, God is proclaimed to be just because He does what He promised He would do, that is, He acts in accordance with the totality of His being and His previous contacts with men. Specifically, this means that He comes forth to save His people.[8] It is only when at times it seems that He is failing to do so that His justice is questioned. As the prophet Isaiah says, for God to be just is to be the Saviour (43:3).

Even though at times Paul speaks of the manifestation of God's righteousness as bringing about the justification of sinners in such a way that they now find themselves in a new condition, his purpose is not to emphasize justification as a condition. That people are accounted just, or declared just, is viewed by Paul as a consequence of God's own righteous action, that is, the revelation of His righteousness. When speaking of the transferal of righteousness to people, Paul uses a forensic metaphor. But this is a *metaphor*, only used to express the consequences of God's action on behalf of mankind. If one keeps in mind what Paul is doing in these chapters, one is able to avoid the commonly made error of interpreting the notion of righteousness in Romans in purely forensic terms. The forensic metaphor was never intended, neither is it able, to carry so much weight. Paul only wishes to affirm that God's action in Christ is the revelation of his righteousness, or justice, because through it God is doing what he promised, that is, what He is supposed to be doing.[9]

The other word in Paul's thesis that needs to be defined is the word faith. In 1:16 it was stated that "the gospel is the power of God for salvation to every one who has faith." After the long digression in which Paul explains that God's righteousness is revealed in the context of God's wrath (1:18-3:20), Paul restates the thesis in 3:21f.: "But now the righteousness of God has been manifested . . . through faith in Jesus Christ for all who believe." What does Paul understand faith to be?

Within the pages of the New Testament the word faith is used differently by different writers. Most striking is the difference to be noted in the ways James and Paul use the word. The well-known chapter eleven of the Epistle to the Hebrews uses the word with connotations of its own, and the Pastoral Letters and Ephesians have yet other meanings for the word. Briefly these meanings may be described as follows:

In the Epistle of James faith means to consent to the truth of a proposition. If one were to say "God is one," anyone who agrees with the statement may be called a believer. But, of course, when faith is understood as "belief," then even "the devils believe and shudder" (James 2:19). When used in this way it is quite clear that faith is not considered to be enough as a mark of discipleship. Works, such as "to visit the orphans, and widows in their affliction, and to keep oneself unstained from the world" (James 1:27), must supplement belief so that religion may have a foundation and relevance in daily life. It would seem that the Epistle of James was in part written to argue against a misreading of Paul, to a degree caused by a failure to understand Paul's use of the word faith. It may be added here that what James calls "works" Paul describes as the "fruit of the Spirit." As will become clear below, by "works of law" Paul has something completely different in mind.

The well-known definition of faith as "the assurance of things hoped for, the conviction of things not seen" (Hebrews 11:1) fully agrees with the theme of the Epistle to the Hebrews. The whole of this epistle is a long exhortation, interrupted by bits of theological observations on the basis of the past history of the people of Israel and their foundational experience at the Exodus. The exhortation could be condensed to the following brief statement: "The journey of life seems long and full of trials and sufferings; therefore, the temptation to give up on God may be quite strong at times, but the reward at the end of the road is such that it makes the whole trip worth while. Keep on; don't falter. If by chance you stumble, don't give up. Get back on your feet and go. Having participated in the march is nothing. Reaching the goal is everything. Faith is what allows you to anticipate the rewards of the end while still on the journey." In Hebrews, faith is associated with patience (6:12). It allows one to anticipate a reality now invisible.

In the Pastoral Letters and in the letter to the Ephesians, faith is used to refer to what Christians believe in. In other words, the body of Christian teachings is the faith. This usage serves at the very beginning of I Timothy to characterize the recipient as a "true child in the faith" (1:2) and then to contrast the true doctrine that has to do with God's redemptive work over against the "myths and endless genealogies which promote speculation" rather than "the faith" (1:4). Likewise, in the formula "One Lord, One Faith, One Baptism" (Ephesians 4:5), faith is used to designate the body of distinctive Christian doctrines which true Christians hold with a good conscience (I Tim. 3:9).

In all the writings of the New Testament faith may be spoken of as a Christian characteristic. Thus the author may congratulate the readers because their faith is strong or is well known beyond the confines of their local community (Rom. 1:8; Eph. 1:15; II Tim. 3:10; Heb. 13:7; James 1:3). These general references to faith, as if it were a Christian virtue, do not help us to decide what is the characteristic meaning of the word for Paul.

When Paul speaks of righteousness by faith it is clear that he is not using the word faith in any of the ways described above. If "Abraham believed and it was counted to him as righteousness," Paul does not see the matter the same way James does (James 2:23). For James, Abraham had faith when he offered his son Isaac as a sacrifice (James 2:21). For Paul, Abraham had faith when he received God's promise (Rom. 4:13), before Isaac was born, before either of them was circumcised (Rom. 4:10). Clearly for Paul faith cannot be a human virtue, a work (Rom. 4:2f.). If faith "works," it is not in order to establish a person's claim to salvation. If it works at all, it is because God's promise is being fulfilled. The work of faith does not have as its object to satisfy the demands of the law or gain ground before God. Rather it is possible for faith to work only by the power of God (II Thess.1:11). It is only "in Christ Jesus" that "faith works through love" (Gal. 5:6) in the extension of salvation to all mankind.

What, then, does Paul mean by faith? To have faith is to trust God's promise and to let him accomplish salvation.[10] Righteousness by faith is salvation by God's action. Faith is the demonstration by a life that the person is no longer atoning for past sins but trusting God's power to live a new life in joy and peace. Righteousness and salvation are synonymous terms for Paul. Compare the contrast between wrath and righteousness in Rom. 1:17, 18 with the contrast between wrath and salvation in I Thess. 5:9. In other words, salvation by faith is God doing his work and men and women trusting that God has done it. To know that God is doing his job, when his job is to save his own creation, is to know that one does not have to insult God by pretending to be doing what God somehow has so far failed to do. To live in this knowledge is the life of obedience, which for Paul is the essence of faith (Rom. 1:5; 16:26). The Pauline admonition "as you have always obeyed, so now, . . . work out your own salvation with fear and trembling" (Phil. 2:12) is not a denial of his doctrine of salvation by faith. Rather, it is the pithy expression of what has been described in the preceding paragraphs. Paul is not contradicting the exalted picture of Christ drawn by the words of the hymn quoted in Philippians 2:6-11. The obedience of the Philippians is not to annul the obedience of Christ described in the hymn. Their fear and trembling is not to be the result of their lack of certainty as to God's estimate of their lives. Their working out of their salvation is not their effort to earn it from God. What is important here is the direction to which the Philippians are being pointed toward by the "therefore, my beloved." The "therefore" that follows the hymn in praise of what Christ has done does not argue that the Philippians must now try their best to please God in order to attain "their own salvation." No. The "therefore" tells them to go forth in the knowledge of what Christ has done and to live with each other in joy and peace in humility, in the mind of Christ. The working out of their salvation is not to be done *vis à vis* God, but *vis à vis* each other in community (2:2-4) and as "one spirit" and "one mind" *vis à vis* their opponents in the world (1:27-28). It is as they strive "side by side for the faith of the gospel" (Phil 1:27) that in their lives they "work out," that is to say confirm, their own salvation, which, of course, God has already accomplished for them (Phil 1:28; 2:13).

Finally, in 3:21, Paul returns to his thesis and begins to develop its first statement. As the power of God working out mankind's salvation, the Gospel is the revelation of God's righteousness (1:17). First of all, he now adds that this revelation takes place without the benefit of the law, even if not in contradiction to what the law might have revealed about God.

This explicit denial of any participation by the law in the

revelation of God's righteousness must, of necessity, be understood as addressed to Jews who may have considered the law the very place where God's righteousness is revealed. For Paul God's wrath and righteousness are revealed concretely in the people who receive them. Just as God's wrath is revealed when He "gives up" people to ever deeper degradation, so also God's righteousness is revealed in the people who receive from God the free gift of salvation after they have believed in Jesus Christ. Thus, Jesus was the one "put forward" by God as the *locus* of propitiation where a meeting between God and people could take place (3:24-26). It is essential to note that for Paul God's righteousness is not known by man as a quality God happens to have. God's righteousness may be seen only in people who have been justified. Now, just as God's wrath is revealed in both Jews and Gentiles who sin--and they all do--so also God's righteousness may be seen in Jews and Gentiles who are justified--and they both may be if they believe in Christ (3:29, 30). Does this mean that the Jew does not have a key to God's house? Yes, it does (3:27). Does this mean that the Jewish law is worthless, or irrelevant, in every way? No, it does not (3:31). Yet it is already clear that the law is not what makes God cease from revealing his wrath and instead reveal his righteousness.[11]

Elaborating on this notion, Paul turns to the story of Abraham. For him it is important to show that God's righteousness came to Abraham as a gift (4:4). Since at the time when Abraham received God's gift he was yet uncircumcised, the gift of salvation may be received by both circumcised and uncircumcised, just as Abraham received it at both stages of his life. This means, then, that the heirs of the gift are those who like Abraham trust God (4:5), and not those who by works of law may feel that they have a right to the gift. A gift may not be earned. If it has been earned it ceases to be a gift and becomes wages for services rendered (4:4).

With the early Christian formula "put to death for our trespasses and raised for our justification" (4:25), Paul comes to the end of his development of the thesis. He seems to be satisfied that by now every reader must have understood that the revelation of the righteousness of God outshines the revelation of God's wrath against the "wickedness of men" (1:18). Basic to the thesis has been the notion that both God's wrath and his righteousness are manifest by the way they work themselves out in concrete human beings and that this has taken place among both Jews and Gentiles, since God "shows no partiality" (2:11).

GOD'S RIGHTEOUSNESS AND THE HUMAN CONDITION

The next section of the epistle represents an attempt to work out some of the corollaries that follow from the thesis. The "therefore" with which Chapter 5 begins represents a logical sequence, "since we are justified by faith, we have peace with God" (5:1). In other words, it is the event of Jesus Christ that changes the human condition from one exemplifying God's wrath to one revealing God's righteousness.

The passage from "wrath" to "peace" does not mean a change of God, or a change in God, but rather it represents a change in the condition of people before God, brought about by God's grace "in which we stand" (5:2). This grace pours out God's love to human hearts by the work of the Holy Spirit and allows men and women now to rejoice in hope (5:2-5). They may rest assured that, no matter what the tribulations of life prove to be, while they are yet "helpless," "ungodly" (5:6), "sinners" (5:8), and "enemies" (5:10), the unheard-of happened and Christ died for them. This means that those who "were reconciled to God by his death" are also saved by his resurrection (5:9f.).

Many theological edifices have been built on the foundation of Romans 5. Most famous of them all is the doctrine of original sin. According to it, in Romans 5 Paul proves that men and women are sinners and are born already stained by the spot of sin on account of the sin committed by Adam. Thus Adam's sin is the sin of all the race that descended from him, and his many descendants have only served to proliferate the sin that Adam brought into the world. As a result, on account of Adam's sin all men die.

For anyone who has been reading the epistle from the beginning, that Paul should say this now would seem redundant at best. Has not Paul already established the universality of sin in chapters 2 and 3? Has he not already clearly stated that God's wrath affects all sinners and that all mankind "has sinned" and "fallen short of the glory of God" (3:23)? By contrast does not chapter 5 begin with the affirmation that on account of the revelation of God's righteousness people have been justified and now rejoice in the hope of "sharing the glory of God" (5:2)? Certainly, Paul does not need to prove again the universality of sin, and the context now is about sharing glory with Christ, rather than sin with Adam.

It is important to note that when Paul brings out the figure of Adam he does not do this in order to prove the universality of sin. Rather, he does it in order to put into high relief the efficacy of what God did in Christ, by contrasting it to what Adam had done.[12] In a sense, Adam serves here only as the negative being used to get a picture of the significance of Christ. In this way Adam was a type of the one to come (5:14). But in another sense, Adam and Christ are contrasted as two orders within which certain conditions obtain. It is obvious, however, that the two orders are not equal. After all, one is the result of Adam's work, while the other is the result of God's activity. If one were to compare the work of Adam and the work of God, one would have to say that God's work should bring about results that are much more lasting and effective than those produced by Adam's work. Paul's point is quite simple. No one can doubt the effectiveness of Adam's work. Through Adam and his sin death entered the world and death, once inside, has been in control of human life ever since. The universality of death is the result of the universality of sin and it proves the effectiveness of Adam's action of allowing sin "to enter" the world. In this way Adam is the "creator" of the "fallen" world. But God's wrath has been replaced by God's righteousness; man's sin has been replaced by God's grace. The reign of death has been replaced by the reign of life (5:17); trespasses have been replaced by obedience. All this has been accomplished by the radical substitution of one order of existence for another.

Adam's world is all too familiar to everyone. It is the order of existence where sinning takes place and where death reigns. Of its reality we have no doubt. Of the conditions of life in it and the inevitability of death in it, we are certain. That another order of existence is a reality within reach for men and women we seem to be less certain. The conditions of life and death in this other order appear to be not well known. Some may think of it as no more than a mirage produced by the will to escape from the order of Adam in which human life goes on. But for Paul the opposite is the case. He argues his point by the repeated use of the formula "if . . . how much more . . ." (5:10, 15, 17, cf.5:9). The general argument could be paraphrased as, "If what Adam did brought results, how much more what Christ did brings even greater results," or, "If in the order of Adam such and such conditions obtain, how much more in the order of Christ these other conditions obtain." Again, "If the results of Adam's work meant this kind of situation, how much more the results of the work of Christ means this other kind of situation."

What Paul is concerned to show here is not that people are sinners (he already did that in 1:18-3:19), but that the revelation of God's righteousness that brings peace and life to mankind creates for men and women an order of existence that is much more real than the order of existence they take for real. After all, the reality of the rule of sin and death in the order of Adam may not be taken as the last word that can be said about God's creation. Paul does not elucidate here the origin of sin or argue for the universality of death. Here he is stating the ever-surpassing reality of the order of righteousness and life over the order of sin and death.

Between Adam and Christ Paul sees some similarities: both accomplished something that had transcendental significance for all mankind. In both cases "one" established conditions that are the reality that "many" (read "all") live. Disobedience translated itself into sinners and obedience has been translated into righteous ones (5:19). More significant than the similarities, however, are the differences. In the first place, there is a marked contrast between the conditions in which humanity finds itself on account of Adam's deed and those brought about by Christ's action. Adam opened the door that allowed sin "to enter" the world. Paul has here personified sin as a power that enters the world of humans and once inside exercises control over them. As a result every one since Adam has sinned and died. Here two things may be noted. One is that Paul makes clear that everyone dies on account of his/her own sin (5:12). The other is that sin existed and controlled human action even before the entrance of the law at Sinai. This means that the death of sinners was not brought about by the condemnation of the law but by the power of sin. By contrast, God's action in Christ brought life to this world. Now those who lived oppressed by the reign of sin and death may reign in life (5:17). In the second place, there is a significant contrast between the logic that argues that sin is to be punished and the lack of logic that argues that everyone's sin results in the justification of all (5:16). Precisely here is where God's grace makes it impossible to compare the act of Adam with the act of Christ. There is nothing comparable to God's grace.

But the over-abundance of God's grace does not flow within the order of sin and death. It flows in an order of its own. It has its own realm of operation. Grace does not work in the kingdom of death. Grace works in the kingdom of life. Therefore, those who are to benefit from the overabundance of grace at work in the Gospel of Jesus Christ must be transferred out of Adam's order and into Christ's order where God's righteousness is at work.

This is God's love. Love is what reaches out and takes the sinner out of the realm of death and brings him into the realm of life (5:8-10). This transferal out of one order, or realm, into the other is possible because in his love God built a bridge. Or maybe it would be accurate to say, God broke the power of the sovereign of the realm of sin and death and thus provided a way of escape out of the realm of death and into the realm of life. The termination of the control that death had over everyone and the way of escape out of the realm of death were accomplished by the death and the resurrection of Jesus Christ. That is the function of the cross, and in that way the cross is the manifestation of God's love at work.[13]

God's grace could have established a realm where God's righteousness was at work and where life reigned, but that realm would have remained uninhabited and desolate, because it was impossible for man to escape from the controlling power of the king of death. If men and women were ever to inhabit the kingdom of life, the kingdom of death had to be stormed and conquered, or at least its power had to be somewhat broken and a way of escape out of it created by someone stronger than the keepers of the gates of the kingdom of death. That is what Christ's cross did. It opened up a breach in the wall of the kingdom of death and sin, and "saved men and women from God's wrath" (5:9). Christ's life, that is, his resurrection, creates the kingdom of grace wherein men and women may live rejoicing in the hope of sharing the glory of God.

As far as Paul is concerned, this cosmic operation into the kingdom of death and the creation of the kingdom of life took place once and for all at the death and the resurrection of Jesus Christ.[14] Romans 5 speaks of the superiority of the realm of grace over the realm of sin. Romans 6 speaks of the way in which individuals make the transfer from one to the other. Believers accomplish the cosmic journey from one realm to the other at baptism. In it they join Christ in his death and resurrection and in this way leave the realm of death and enter the realm of life. Christ's death and resurrection is an accomplished fact firmly established by witnesses among which Paul counts himself (I Cor. 15:5-8). Christians who are baptized do not reproduce Christ's death and resurrection; neither do they appropriate the benefits of his death and resurrection. Rather, they in fact participate in it and as a result they move out of Adam's world in order to enter Christ's world. That is the only way to accomplish this transferral, which, as the apostle sees it, is indispensable for the Christian life.

To understand Christianity in a Pauline sense one must grasp the primary significance of his vision of the two realms, or orders of being that have existed side by side since the cross of Christ. Outside of Christ there is only one order, one set of human possibilities, and one final outcome--the manifestation of God's wrath. By the cross of Christ a new order has been opened up with a different set of human possibilities and a contrasting final outcome: the revelation of God's righteousness.

Life in the order of Adam was life "enslaved to sin" (6:6). But death with Christ through baptism is freedom from sin (6:7). He who lives by grace, therefore, is no longer in the reign of sin (6:12). He has moved out and found a new life in the reign of life and righteousness. As Paul sees it, human life is always lived under the domain of a sovereign ruler. Freedom is not an absolute, meaningful by itself. Freedom must be established in reference to concrete options. As Paul sees it, in the order of Adam one is free *from* righteousness and free *to* sin (6:20), but in the order of Christ one is free *from* sin and free *for* God (6:18).

The fact that in both realms, or orders, one is a slave, may induce some to think that it makes no difference in what order one lives one's life. In either one servitude is the mode of life. This similarity is only apparent. In terms of the quality of life and the final outcome the contrast could not be greater. Whereas in one, life is a yielding "to impurity and to greater and greater iniquity" as God gives up men and women and makes them fit for his wrath

(6:19a), in the other, life is a yielding to righteousness that brings
forth sanctification (6:19b). It is clear that here Paul contrasts the
sinking of mankind into iniquity as a manifestation of God's wrath,
with the uplifting of mankind into sanctification as a manifestation of God's righteousness, whose final outcome is eternal life
(6:22). In the final formula of the chapter it would seem that by
distinguishing "wages" from "free gifts" Paul is contrasting the one
who pays wages and the one who gives gifts. These two words
only contrast the way in which humans receive death and life.
They receive life as a gift, but death as wages. They earn death by
their sinning, but they can only be given life as a gift, unearned.
Whether as wages or as gift, whatever they receive, ultimately
they receive it from God.

So far, a significant element in Paul's presentation of the
Gospel has been purposely left out. Paul is writing to a Roman
community of Christians who, like all Christians of the 50's, still
see the Christian Gospel as a development within the Jewish phenomenon. At the center of the Jewish faith, ever since the formation of the first Jewish commonwealth after the Maccabean War and
the formation of the canon, was the law. It had been codified to
serve as a kind of constitution for the life of those who had been
trying since the return from the exile to live as a religiously
oriented society. In their efforts to give divine sanction to their
socio-political arrangements, the Jews had given the law divine
status. Now it was claimed that it had existed from eternity, and
it would continue to be the basis for the conduct of life in the
age to come.[15] Not only the Rabbis, whose pronouncements were
collected in the Mishna, claimed divine authority for the law and
presupposed its eternal validity. The best known diaspora Jew of
the first century, Philo of Alexandria, also made the law the supreme revelation of God to humanity. Its message had to be taken
with utmost seriousness since it is the supreme expression of
wisdom.[16]

As A Christian Paul has come to a radical reappraisal of the
eternal nature of the law. As he sees it, prior to Moses there was
no law (Rom. 5:13f.) and with Christ the supremacy of the law had
come to an end (Rom.10:4). As Paul makes clear, the existence of
sin is not dependent on the existence of the law. When the law
entered the world through Moses, the world was already in sub-
mission to sin due to Adam's act. After the death of Christ even

Christians who have through baptism joined him in the death of the old world of sin still find themselves, as long as they live in this fallen creation that waits for the Parousia, subject to sinning. But for them the power of condemnation inherent in the law has been broken (Rom. 8:1). Chapter 7 analyzes the strenuous situation that is experienced by Christians who have died with Christ to sin and death, in as much as they still live in their bodies, in this natural world. They find themselves still subject to the power of the law that since Moses has served not only to establish sin (Rom. 5:20), but also to awaken dormant sin which has found a lodging for itself in "the body" (Rom. 7:7-10). Thus the coming of the law rather than put an end to sin only served to make sin more abundant. In the realm of flesh the commandment that was holy, good and spiritual (7:12, 14) only serves to condemn the sinner to death. The Chapter's conclusion, "Thanks be to God for his inexpressible gift" in Christ who actually delivers from "the body of death," is not an autobiographical climax to Paul's career as a Jew or as a Christian.[17] What the last verses of the chapter describe is the eschatological tension of all Christian existence that knows of the proper role of the law and the significance of the death and resurrection of Christ and yet finds itself somehow overpowered by a law that only rules in sin and death over those who still live in bodies. The eschatological tension of "life between the times" is characteristic of Christians who are no longer under the law but not yet in the Kingdom of the Father.

Chapter 8 starts with the positive assertion that "there is, therefore, no condemnation for those who are in Christ Jesus." Why? Because those who are in Christ Jesus are no longer within the realm in which the law is operative. Paul repeatedly stresses the point that the law has its limits. Someone living in France does not live under the jurisdiction of the laws of the United States but rather under the laws of France. Paul exemplifies this same notion by the analogy of the married woman (7:2-3). While her husband is alive, she is bound to him; when her husband dies, she is free from him. The same is true of men and women. While they live in Adam, they are bound to the law that brought condemnation for their sins. When they die with Christ to the world of Adam, they enter the realm of Christ and they are free *from* the "law of sin and death," but they are free *for* the "law of the spirit of life" (8:2). The difference between these two laws is that whereas one functioned to objectify sin and brought about death, the other functions to strengthen our weakness (8:26) and aids in seeking God as our only strength, teaching us to say "abba, abba" (8:15). Paul has thus come to the final question, What then shall we say to this? If God is for us who is against us? If God's wrath and the wages of our sin are no longer our due, then God's right-eousness has done its work in providing the gift of life for us. What else is there? This is God's world, no one else's. Nothing can prevent God's love from storming the reign of death and prevent Him from transferring us to the reign of life. Paul's argu-ment seems complete.

GOD'S FAITHFULNESS

Yet again, as in 2:1 and 7:1 Paul recognizes the problem all this represents for the Jews who have been trained to think in a particular way. Paul has, therefore, some very pertinent things to say to his "brethren and kinsmen by race" (9:3). This next section of the letter (9:1-11:36) is an attempt on the part of Paul to answer any possible objections that Jews might have against his thesis. The whole of Paul's argument is based on the notion that God is righteous, that is, that he is a promise-keeping God. In other words, God is faithful.

It would appear, however, that if what Paul has said is true, God's faithfulness may be called into question. As the Jews might see it, the God preached by Paul would seem to be capricious. If this Gospel is true, has not God been unfaithful to Israel? Has not the word of God failed? (9:6). How can Israel's privileged status *vis à vis* the Gentiles be annulled willy-nilly without a redefinition of the character of God? If God has indeed failed in his promises to Israel, then what guarantees do Christians have that tomorrow God will not change things around again and leave them on a limb ready to be cut for firewood? If the thesis is to be maintained, God's faithfulness in Christ must be related to the history of Israel and to her life under the law.

Paul now launches an apology on behalf of God's faithfulness by making three points. Sometimes this apology has been construed as a Christian philosophy of history or as a theodicy,[18] but Paul's aim seems to be much less pretentious. In fact, his aim seems to be rather practical. It may very well be that these words, while taking account of the position of Jews *vis à vis* the Gospel also have to do with the actual historical circumstances that prompted Paul to write this letter in the first place. That this is, in fact, the general thrust of the letter is also supported by 15:7f., as will be made clear below.

The first argument in Paul's apology is to establish the connection between God's promises and Israel's election (9:6-29). The Old Testament says (9:7) that the promise made to Abraham was not effective in all his descendants. Thus, the election of Abraham does not mean that all his descendants are heirs automatically, cf. Ishmael and his descendants, Esau and his, etc. Election has always been dynamic within history. As the creator, God has absolute power and control over his creation. His election is not a static choice made once but a continuous unfolding of his will according to his wrath and his mercy (9:22f.). Hosea and Isaiah testify to that (9:25-29). Can we, his creatures, charge God with injustice? By no means! (9:14, 19, 20).

The second argument made by Paul is that if Israel now finds itself no longer in its old privileged position, the cause for such a state of affairs has not been God's unfaithfulness but Israel's misguided attachment to the law (9:30-10:21). The insistent search for righteousness by means of works of law has consistently failed those Jews trying to reach it thusly, while, in comic reversal, the Gentiles, who did not strive after it, have attained to it (9:30). Their unwillingness to accept God's freedom in history has prevented many Israelites from coming to know "the righteousness that comes from God" (10:3). God's purpose to save sinners, however, remains ever the same, even if Christ is the end of the law as a means to attain to righteousness (10:4). Still, if a Jew wishes to be a child of the promise, "the opportunity is near" (10:8). Jews are not being asked to do the impossible, like storming heaven above or the abyss below, in order to find out what righteousness by faith is all about. All they have to do is to receive the word which messengers of the Gospel are proclaiming everywhere, but as in the time of Isaiah "they have not all heeded the Gospel" (10:16).

The third point is an argument from common sense (11:1-12). It cannot be said that God is unfaithful to Israelites because as Paul says, "I am an Israelite." Paul is a living example that God has not rejected his people (11:1). It has always been the case that God has kept a remnant with whom his promise remained in effect. That the majority of the people have not accepted that God's salvation is taking place apart from the law does not prove God's bad faith. It only makes those people subject to God's wrath. It may very well be that the failure of Israel to believe, which has made room for the Gentiles, will ultimately serve to make Israel jealous. Thus Israel's failure has meant riches for the world at large, and Israel's conversion will mean an even greater distribution of God's riches in the world (11:12).

So far Paul has been counterbalancing possible objections on the part of Jews. Now Paul interrupts his apology on behalf of God's righteousness and explains to the Gentiles in the Roman church their position *vis à vis* the Jews in the overall working out of salvation for mankind by the power of the Gospel. These words addressed to the Gentiles (11:15-26) have a very clear aim in view. They are intended to prevent the Gentiles from boasting about the fact that they, on account of God's grace, even though not following after righteousness, have attained it (9:30). It is to make this point to his Gentile brethren that Paul uses the metaphor of the holy root (11:16). The Gentiles, who are branches from a wild root, have been grafted into the holy root, some of whose own branches have been cut. As grafted branches they must not forget their origin, neither must they forget that they are receiving nourishment from the holy root. Moreover, it is well within God's power to graft back into the holy root the very branches that he once had cut off. As a final word, Paul tells them that as a matter of fact, they have no ground for pride because at the end "all Israel will be saved" (11:26). Grafting, after all, was a process used to save old olive trees.[19]

Nowhere is Paul's identification with his Jewish brethren more in evidence than here. It would seem that he has forgotten his argument about the dynamic nature of election within history, which allows for some of the children of the elect to be rejected in the course of time. Now Paul says "as regards election they are beloved for the sake of their forefathers. For the gifts and the call of God are irrevocable" (11:28, 29). It would seem, then, that the lack of faith on the part of Gentiles, or of Jews, at different moments in history are ultimately annulled by the grace of God that aims "to have mercy on all" (11:32). Paul's confidence on God's grace is based on two considerations: God's mercy and the merits of the forefathers. The doctrine of the merits of the fathers, well known by the Pharisees of the time, affirmed that in spite of the sins of the present generation God will have mercy on Israel "for the sake of the forefathers."[20] This vision of universal salvation, that found expression in Israel since the time of the Exile, causes Paul to desist from arguing as to how to understand God's dynamic ways in history and take flight in the words of poetry. He quotes a hymn that praises Wisdom by declaring its judgments "unsearchable" and its ways "past finding out" (9:33). God has pronounced a "Yes" to humanity and as a consequence both Jews and Gentiles must allow God's Wisdom to work things out without pretending to understand how God finally accomplishes all things since "of him, and through him, and to him, are all things." This exuberant, all-inclusive vision of God's grace and wisdom bringing about His ultimate purpose cannot be understood in isolation. It does not follow from it that God's grace overrides the lack of faith on the part of some in order to bring about universal salvation. The action of God in Christ is universal inasmuch as it affects everyone in all creation, but participation in God's life is dependent on faith in what God has done.[21] With the doxology, "To Him be glory for ever. Amen" (11:36), the presentation, the corollaries, and the explications of the initial thesis come to an end.

THE CHRISTIAN LIFE

Following the full elaboration of the thesis is a series of practical admonitions for the Christian life (12:1-15:13), which serve rhetorically to give weight to his message in view of his plans for a future visit to Rome. These are followed by some autobiographical information and travel plans (15:14-33) and the epistolary conclusion demanded by usage.

It is to be noted, however, that the series of hortatory remarks are certainly integral to the purpose of the letter. If they are not commented upon here it is not because they should be considered unimportant. In the chapters that follow there shall be an opportunity to comment on some of Paul's remarks. Their presence in the letter to the Romans argues for the view that Paul did not think of the Gospel as just an intellectual exercise. Even if he lived in the expectation of the imminent Parousia, he did not think for a moment that life in human society was, therefore, unworthy of careful consideration. For him the Gospel made sense precisely on account of the way it affected everyday life. In this he was a true son of the Pharisees. They, too, thought of religion as something making a difference in the way one lived.

A clue to what was uppermost in Paul's mind when he wrote the letter may be found in the transition from the exhortations to the concluding section where he rehearses his future travel plans. It would seem that Paul has already begun to close the letter, but before concluding he wants to underline what it has been all about. It is a well-known rhetorical device recommended by teachers since time began: repeat. First, you tell them what you are going to tell them (1:16, 17), then you tell them (1:18-15:6), then you tell them what you told them (15:7-9).

The practical admonitions (12:1-15:13) end with two petitions: "May the God of steadfastness and encouragement grant you to live in such harmony with one another, in accord with Christ Jesus, that together you may with one voice glorify the God and Father of our Lord Jesus Christ" (15:5f.) and "May the God of hope fill you with all joy and peace in believing, so that by the power of the Holy Spirit you may abound in hope" (15:13). Between these two petitions Paul recapitulates and brings in four Old Testament quotations to substantiate his point. It is clear that 15:8f. is a restating of 1:16. There the apostle said ". . . the gospel is the power of God for salvation to every one who has faith, to the Jew first and also to the Greek." Now he reaffirms, "Christ became a servant to the circumcised to show God's truthfulness, in order to confirm the promise given to the patriarchs, and in order that the Gentiles might glorify God for his mercy." The sentence is not perfectly balanced because in Paul's mind there is always present the fact that "first" God did something for the Jews. But Paul also restates that what God has done *now* was done "once for all to confirm the promise to the patriarchs." God's salvation for all is his promise-keeping righteousness. The sentence does wish to establish a balance between the salvation of the Jews and the salvation of the Gentiles "on account of God's truth." In order to keep covenant with the patriarchs, Christ became a servant to the Jews, but on account of God's mercy even his servanthood among the Jews was carried out with a view that the Gentiles might glorify God for the salvation he had brought to mankind. Thus

Jews and Gentiles must live "in harmony, in peace and joy in believing" waiting upon the God of steadfastness, encouragement and hope. His steadfastness has been demonstrated in the death and resurrection of Christ. His encouragement is the present comfort of the church, and hope is her future.

Paul concludes his letter greeting by name a rather large number of people whom he had come to know elsewhere, but who are now living in Rome.[22] That Paul should have so many acquaintances in a city where he had not been before has been understood to indicate that the greetings found at the end of the letter to the Romans did not belong to the original letter. In that case the greetings were addressed by Paul to a church he had established, where he knew the members well. This explanation is not necessary, however, since the list may be understood to exemplify the great mobility possible within the Roman Empire. This mobility was not a particularly Christian characteristic, but that so many Christians were engaging in so much traveling signifies that they were not poor agricultural workers bound to the land, but rather members of the urban middle class engaged in manual trades or commerce. Many Christians seem to have freely taken advantage of this facility for traveling enjoyed by purchasing agents, salespeople, artisans, professionals, and others in the Roman empire. That they were traveling widely and getting acquainted with other Christians everywhere argues for the fact that Christians were members of the urban lower middle class that flourished under the *pax romana*.[23]

CHAPTER IV

THE CROSS AND THE END

To an unbiased observer, if the crucifixion of Jesus was at all related to God it could only show the weakness of God (1 Cor. 1:25). A God who cannot prevent the death of His son does not seem powerful at all. Moreover, if it were argued that to accomplish mankind's salvation the spilling of blood was necessary, nothing could demand a crucifixion. Crucifixion was the most degrading of deaths, and it was understood as such by both Jews and Gentiles.[1] As far as the Jews were concerned, to be hung on a cross or tree, either before or after one's death, was a clear indication of divine condemnation. In the Old Testament period, after blasphemers had been stoned to death they were hanged in order to make public their rejection by God and the people. It appears that certain Jews under some circumstances in the first and second centuries B.C.E. also hanged blasphemers before their death in order to increase their torture and public rejection.[2] No Old Testament passage ever considers the possibility that one who is to fulfill a divine mission on earth could possibly end up crucified. Isaiah's picture of the suffering servant makes clear the servant's sufferings and even death, but no crucifixion is envisaged. No agent of God could be cursed in this way by God himself. To the Jew the cross was certainly a "stumbling block" (I Cor. 1:23, Rom. 9:32f.).

In the Gentile world, matters were not much different. Crucifixion was not the public demonstration of a divine curse on the one who so suffered in disgrace. It was rather the form of death reserved for the lowest classes, primarily traitors and slaves. No matter what his crime no Roman with social standing, or even a captured enemy of some prominence, could be hanged on a cross. This was reserved for men without social rank.[3] After all, the cross by itself was not an instrument for death. Rather it was an instrument of torture. Torture applied for a sufficient length of time would inevitably lead to death, but the cross was actually only secondarily related to the cause of death. Medically speaking, he who dies on a cross dies on account of the collapse of the diaphragm, an involuntary muscle that pumps air into the lungs.[4]

This shameful and cruel death by torture was certainly distasteful and ignominious to the Gentiles. Roman men and women of the higher classes, when condemned for serious crimes, would be ordered to commit suicide. The actual means left to the discretion of the one being punished. Usually they elected either to take some poison that worked quickly or painlessly, or they prepared a warm bath and had a doctor open their veins so that the blood would flow into the warm water. Death would then come easily as a debilitating stupor. Criminals of the middle classes would be decapitated by an executioner. According to tradition that was the way in which Paul himself met death.[5] But Jesus of Nazareth, a poor Galilean with a messianic following, was crucified. It could very well have been the case that the Jewish authorities sought a crucifixion for Jesus in order to insure that his followers would abandon their messianic dreams about him.[6] The documents make clear that in this the Jewish leaders succeeded. It is also clear that after the crucifixion and the entombment the disciples thought their expectation had been mistaken and decided to go back to Galilee to reopen their fishing business.[7]

THE CROSS AS ESCHATOLOGICAL EVENT

The resurrection proved that the cross had not been the end of the life of Jesus. It demanded a re-evaluation of the cross. Understood as part of God's action on behalf of mankind, the cross did not mean the end of Jesus. It meant the end of the fallen world brought about by Adam's disobedience. If the resurrection is the creation of new life in the spirit, the cross is the destruction of all life in the flesh. For Paul the cross demonstrated the power of God at work in bringing the fallen world and all its values and standards to an end. The old had been destroyed: behold, all things have been made new. Paul understood this clearly, and dedicated his life to proclaim the fact that human life on earth was no longer limited by its mortality. A new way of life had been opened up for all men and women by the death and resurrection of Christ.

This had been God's doing on behalf of mankind.[8]

The cross of Christ may have been a stumbling block to Jews and folly to Gentiles, but to Paul it was the manifestation of God's power and wisdom. In it God had effectively destroyed the power of sin over mankind. Paul was not speculating; he was talking on the basis of his own experience and the experience of those who had responded to his preaching. As a historical occurrence the cross was an event that actually happened outside Jerusalem. For Paul, this occurrence played a role in a historical sequence of events. The significant moments in the sequence of which the cross marked the end are referred to by Paul as Adam, Abraham, and Moses. Now he adds Christ.[9] But just as Adam, Abraham, and Moses remained effective after their own lives, so also Christ and his cross continue to be effective after the actual event outside Jerusalem was accomplished. The power of God released at the cross and the resurrection of Christ continues to be effective in the world by "the word of the cross." Like the word of God that created the heavens and the earth, now the word of the cross creates a new world (II Cor. 4:6).

The spreading of the word of the cross makes it possible for men and women to experience the power of God destroying and creating their lives (Rom. 10:8-10, 17). Paul is almost incapable of understanding how it was possible for those who heard him preach the word of the cross of Christ in Galatia to think that the power of the cross had left something undone which they had to accomplish by themselves afterwards. Reading Gal. 3:1 one is led to believe that Christ had been crucified in Galatia and the Christians there had been eyewitnesses to the fact. Certainly, Paul is not suggesting such historical distortion. Rather, he is contending that the word of the cross is as effective and as powerful as the cross itself. Therefore, when he preached Christ crucified, for all practical purposes, it was as if his hearers had stood at Golgotha and had witnessed the crucifixion. The Galatians themselves needed no theoretical arguments to prove that they had experienced new life by the preaching of the word of the cross (Gal. 3:2-5). The transformation of their lives had not been accomplished by Paul the preacher but by God who had been active at the Cross and was now active in the ministry of Paul (II Cor. 1:21; 2:14, 17; 3:5f.; 5:18-20; 6:1).

By means of the word of the cross the power of the cross

continues to be effective in the world of men and women. For Paul, the world of Adam was not a personal world. It is not the case that when an individual exercises faith in Christ and his cross another Adam dies. The event of the cross took place once and for all (Rom. 6:10). As a historical event it effectively demonstrated God's power by releasing the hold of the forces of death on humanity. What Christ did on the cross he did once for all and for the benefit of everybody who may ever come to live on this world. The cross was, as it were, a battle in which the forces of evil suffered a decisive defeat. As such the cross marks the end of an era. It put an end to the world in which the forces of evil had been operating rather freely on account of God's wrath. At least since the cross their real intentions can no longer be hidden. Their cunning and deceit have been exposed (II Cor. 2:11, cf. Col. 2:14).

What was accomplished by the power of God at the cross of Christ continues to be accomplished by the power of God in the word of the cross. In this way any one engaged in preaching the Gospel is a "fellow-worker" of God (I Cor. 3:9) who needs to be careful as to how he preaches "lest the cross of Christ be emptied of its power" (I Cor. 1:17). For Paul it is clear that if Christian preaching has power at all it is only as it extends that which was accomplished at the cross. In this way, the very power that was at work at the cross continues to work through Christian preaching and allows for people of distant lands and later generations to participate in what was accomplished on Golgotha, namely, the destruction of the world of sin.[10] No Christian preacher, no matter how eloquent, or wise, or powerful, according to Paul, could ever do that. To make the point he rhetorically asks, "Was Paul crucified for you?" (I Cor. 1:13). To keep ministers of the word of the cross conscious of their own limitations and aware of whose power accomplishes the work they are apparently performing, Paul confesses that the powerful word is a "treasure" carried around in the world by preachers who are by contrast only "earthen vessels" (II Cor. 4:7).

Paul is very clear about how the cross of Christ as historical event put an end to an era. As a result, the release of God's power in the cross and the resurrection, which for Paul are inseparable, also means the opening up of a new era. Yet Paul is not blind to the fact that death continues to operate in the world, sinning goes on, men and women still worship idols and the powers of the universe. Even the Jews who worship the true God continue to deal with God on the basis of the Mosaic laws. For all intents and purposes life on earth after the cross and the resurrection seems no different from what it had been before. Certainly, Paul was not unaware of this obvious fact. Yet how could he still claim that the cross marked an end? The answer to this question is not simple.

THE APOCALYPTIC FRAMEWORK

As said already, Paul thought apocalyptically. Among other things, this means that he thought in terms of eras or ages. Basically, there were two ages: This Age and The Age to Come.[11] Already in apocalyptic Judaism there was room for a transition period between the two Ages.[12] The roots for this apocalyptic perspective are found in prophetic preaching about the Day of the Lord. In the prophets, some day soon the Lord himself will step into history in order to establish justice and faithfulness on earth. In that day the Lord will be recognized as Lord by all the nations, and He will rule in peace from Jerusalem. In the meantime, the Lord is guiding the affairs of the nations through natural and historical agencies, e.g., locusts and Assyrian armies. In other words, there is evil in the world which needs to be punished, and God is doing this through His agencies. When the Day of the Lord comes He will break into history Himself, judge the nations, and life on earth will continue on a new plane of justice, love, and peace.

This basic ground plan of the prophetic preaching was modified by the later prophets and the apocalypticists, on account of their different perception of the extent of evil in the world. The Exile in Babylon (605-538), and life under the oppressive rule of the successors of Alexander the Great (331-312) culminating in the Maccabbean Wars (167-164), forced Jewish theologians to reevaluate the significance of the Day of the Lord. The contrast between what they were experiencing before "that day" and what life was going to be like after "that day" now came to be understood as that between night and day. Thus the prophetic emphasis on the day itself now was transferred to the hope of life after that day. Besides, the transition from before to after the day became so radical that more than just a day would be needed to carry it out. Thus the prophetic Day of the Lord became the apocalyptic Age of Messiah. Still the Age of Messiah was conceived as a rather brief period of time during which the things necessary to bring about the transition from This Age to The Age to Come would be accomplished. Judaism in the centuries around the time of Christ did not have anything close to an established orthodoxy, and apocalypticism, as one of the many ways in which Judaism could be understood, did not have one either. Messianic conceptions varied greatly, and around the central messianic figures there was a great variety of other divine agents supposed to come to accomplish different tasks necessary for the transition from This Age to The Age to Come.

Early Christianity from its very inception seems to have understood the significance of the death and the resurrection of Jesus apocalyptically. It was the clear sign that This Age had come to an end. The Age of Messiah had begun.[13] As Christians understood things, what in prophetic thought had been the Day of the Lord and in apocalyptic thought had become the Age of Messiah had now arrived. In this sense the cross and the resurrection marked the end of an era. The whole period of the ministry of Jesus on earth could, therefore, be referred to as the Day of the Lord.[14]

It is quite clear that Paul sees his own life taking place in the short period known as the Age of Messiah. He expects to be alive when the Age of Messiah gives place to the Age to Come at the Parousia of Jesus Christ (I Thess. 4:17, I Cor. 15:51). His preaching of the word of the cross was the way in which God was reaching out to men and women. He was "an ambassador for Messiah" (II Cor. 5:20). For Paul the cross does not mean the end of the earthly life of Jesus. It means the end of an era. "We are convinced that one has died for all; therefore all have died" (II Cor. 5:14). The death of Christ brings about everyone's death because apocalyptically This Age is over.

Still the Age to Come has not yet begun. Not even the presence of the Spirit on earth is to be understood to mean that Christians are already living in the Age to Come. Apparently, some at Corinth understood things in this way. But Paul in his letters to them makes it quite clear that even though one era has ended the other has not yet begun. The death and the resurrection have marked a decisive step in the process to inaugurate the Age to

Come, but the process is now going on. Christ has taken the Kingdom away from the powers of evil, but men and women are still living in physical, fleshly (i.e., weak) bodies. It is not until the time after those-who-belong-to-Christ receive an incorruptible, immortal, spiritual body that the end comes and Christ "delivers the Kingdom to God the Father after destroying every rule and every authority and power. For he must reign until he has put all his enemies under his feet. The last enemy to be destroyed is death. . . . When all things are subjected to him, then the Son himself will also be subjected to him who put all things under him, that God may be everything to everyone" (I Cor. 15:24-28). These words reflect the early Christian understanding that the cross of Christ was the way in which Christ made an inroad into the world of the powers that had kept humankind enslaved in sin. The resurrection was God's way of exalting Christ above all these powers, without necessarily meaning that Christ had already attained effective control over all of them. The age of Messiah is the time given to Messiah to accomplish the subjugation of the lords of the cosmic spheres.

In order to understand the way in which Paul may have visualized how Jesus' death could mean His conquering of death, but at the same time His going forth to conquer the rulers of the heavenly spheres who still kept human life under their control, one may remember a bit of history that must have been quite well known to all Jews of the first century. After the coming of the Romans to Palestine in the person of Pompey in 63 B.C.E., descendants of the Hasmonean native rulers had been rather ineffective in Jerusalem as High Priests, family intrigues demanding most of their energies. In the meantime, Antipater, Herod's father, and later Herod himself and his brother Phasael had been the Roman watchdogs and informants in the general region between Syria and Egypt. They themselves were, however, Idumeans. In 40 B.C., Antigonus, one of the Hasmoneans, rebelled against Rome. He had the open support of the Parthians, who ruled the lands East of the Euphrates river where a major Jewish community still lived since the time of the Exile. Herod immediately placed his family in the easily defensible fortress at Massada and left for Rome. There the Roman Senate without much hesitation proclaimed him *rex socius* of the Romans (allied King). Technically speaking, from that moment on Herod was King and all his vassals recognized and obliged him as such. Still Herod came back to Palestine and found his enemy Antigonus ruling in Jerusalem. His having been proclaimed King by the Roman senate had not appreciably changed the political realities of Palestine. It took Herod three years of warfare to gain military and political control of the country. Historians still ask themselves whether the reign of Herod began in the year 40 B.C.E., when the Roman Senate proclaimed him king, or in the year 37 B.C.E., when having conquered Antigonus the same Roman Senate gave him permission to execute him (this being the first time a conquered king was ever executed with approval from the Roman Senate).[15]

Undoubtedly, the actual war of conquest had been greatly facilitated by the fact that having been proclaimed King by the Senate, Herod could now command the people as a king. All those who saw their future with Rome, rather than with Parthia eagerly offered to help him to carry out the re-conquest of the countryside and the defeat of Antigonus. This bit of recent history may have given the early Christians a model by which to understand the work that Jesus had accomplished and still needed to carry out. When the war would be over, the forces of evil could be finally executed in a lake of fire (Rev. 20:10, 14). As stylistically portrayed in the hymn quoted by Paul in Philippians 2:6-11, the resurrection was the exaltation of Jesus so that he received "a name that is above every name, that at the name of Jesus every knee should bow." The same is said in the early Christian confession quoted by Paul in the beginning of the letter to the Romans: "The Gospel concerning his Son, who was descended from David according to the flesh and was designated Son of God in power according to the Holy Spirit by the resurrection from the dead, Jesus Christ our Lord" (1:3f.).

Yet his exaltation above every name, or his designation as Son of God by his resurrection, had not materially changed the social, economic, political, cultural, religious, or natural life of men and women on earth. Christ reigns as Son of God and Lord, but he still has to ultimately subjugate every lord, authority, power, and dominion. "He must reign until he has put all his enemies under his feet," including death. When he has done that He himself will place himself, and everything else under His dominion, under the Lordship of God himself. In other words, the preaching of the word of the cross is the way in which the ambassadors of God, who are fellow-workers with Christ, are actually by the power of

God taking possession of the land and destroying the power of the forces of evil. At the Parousia these forces will be ultimately eliminated by Christ "when he delivers the Kingdom to God the Father" (I Cor. 15:24).

We see, then, that the cross is a definite historical moment that accomplished once and for all the triumph over death (II Cor. 4:14). It opened up the only passage through which freedom from the powers that enslave human beings may be attained. In that sense the cross is the end of the rule of the kingdom of sin and death. On the other hand, the powers that enslave men and women in sin and bring about death are still at large in the world, and the effective destruction of their power will not take place until the ultimate destruction of their world at the Parousia. The life of the Risen Christ opened the possibility for men and women to live in Christ. Yet those who live by the power of the resurrection still live in a world that is not free from physical death. Just as the resurrection of Christ brought life to all, so also the cross of Jesus brought about the end of the world of Adam. Yet the destruction of the power of sin will no be total until the Parousia. It is only then that Christ achieves ultimate victory and "delivers the kingdom to God the Father" (I Cor. 15:24) for Him to rule it after everything that ever opposed God's will has been destroyed. Paul's letters fully express his expectations for "that day" (Rom. 13:11-14; I Cor. 1:7; 7:29, 31; 10:11; Phil. 3:20f.; 4:5; I Thess. 4:15), which he redefines as "the day of Christ" (Phil. 1:10).

THE TENSION BETWEEN "ALREADY" AND "NOT YET"

It is significant to notice, however, that for Paul the creation of a new world to replace the world of sin and death does not take place at, or after, the Parousia.[16] It has already taken place at the cross and the resurrection. All this is the work of God. The power of God has already done its creative work. Because of this particular way of seeing the eschatological tension between the *already* of the cross and the resurrection and the *not yet* of the Parousia, it is easy to understand how some of Paul's converts may have failed to see the eschatological tension involved here and may have thought that after baptism they were already living the life of the resurrection. Paul argues against these self-deceived Christians at

Corinth. He makes clear that even though the resurrection of Christ is a reality (I Cor. 15:12-20) and on account of it the resurrection of all believers is also to be a reality (I Cor. 15:21-34), this does not mean that the resurrection of the Christian has already taken place. The official end brought about by the cross of Christ still has to wait until the Parousia for the effective end of death itself (I Cor. 15:42-58).[17]

The Parousia is at the center of the Pauline notion of hope, one of the three basic Christian characteristics (I Cor. 13:12; 15:19), but the Parousia as a work of God is also associated with the wrath of God. On the one hand, Paul sees ahead the day of wrath when all those who reveal God's wrath in their lives will meet God's judgment on their evil-doing (Rom 2:5-11). On the other hand, he sees that believers have been saved from the wrath of God and that, therefore, at the Parousia of the Son of God they will not be subject to God's wrath. Jesus has saved them from the "wrath to come" (I Thess. 1:10). Their destiny is not determined by God's wrath but by God's salvation (I Thess. 5:9).

The ultimate destiny of the believer is not confined to a life of service with Christ full of tribulation, joy, dangers of death, and victories. On earth Paul is a pilgrim living in a tent (II Cor. 5:4). His lack of a permanent dwelling place is not due to his many travels for Christ but to the fact that once baptized into the death and resurrection of Christ his very body is not the real home of his very self. Paul recognizes that as long as he participates in the life of a fallen creation, by the very fact that he still lives in a body that is bound to death (Rom. 7:25), he has not yet attained to the full reality of God's salvation.[18]

To exist in the tension between the life of faith and life in the flesh is the very definition of Christian existence. Thus while struggling with the forces of evil that try to prevent the accomplishment of his mission, Paul at times confesses to have contemplated the apparent bonanza that would be to die and escape from the tensions of existence "between the times" of Christ's cross and Parousia. He could then be with Christ. But the thought is rejected as absurd because if he should (by death) abandon his physical body, his spiritual body would not be given him until the Parousia, and he cannot imagine how "naked" existence without a body, could be any better than existence in a physical body (II Cor. 5:3-4). Thus he would rather wait until the Parousia and then be with Christ in the glorious resurrection body. In the meantime, he has an important task to perform which "the love of Christ compels him" to carry out no matter the circumstances under which he must work. He has been entrusted with announcing God's reconciling of the world unto Himself (II Cor. 5:14-21). In carrying out this task, as a co-worker of Christ, he is collaborating in the bringing about of the salvation of mankind. Since saving mankind is how God manifests His righteousness, when men and women participate in the bringing about of God's salvation to others they "become (agents of) the righteousness of God" (II Cor. 5:21).

Paul hopes to be alive at the Parousia of Jesus Christ. He certainly did not envisage the almost two thousand years of history that have transpired since his day. What the Parousia will bring is full participation in the glory of God (Rom. 5:2). Just as God's glory shines in the face of Jesus Christ (II Cor. 4:6), so also God's glory shall shine in the faces of all those who shall participate in the resurrection body. The resurrection of Jesus was only the first fruits of the harvest which "all those who are Christ's shall receive at his coming" (I Cor. 15:23). The hope of sharing the glory of God in the resurrection body (I Cor. 15:49), is not for Paul a way of escaping an unpleasant earthly existence. Rather, it is a significant, even an essential, element in his vision of what God's justice is all about. His life of toil and suffering for Christ is something he embraces as part of his mission, not something about which he feels powerless. It is carefully balanced against the hope of glory and the redemption of the body (Rom. 5:2f.; 8:17b, 18; II Cor. 4:8f.,14).

The apostle's hope for a life where "mortality has been swallowed up by life" (II Cor. 5:4) is not a palliative administered to his converts to help them endure the hardships of economic and social injustices within the Roman Empire. He was not a "false merchant of the word of God" (II Cor. 2:17). Christians at times may have used the Christian message of hope in order to maintain an economic or social order in which they had vested interests, but Paul can not be charged with that. Neither can he be charged with having presented the eschatological hope as an escape from the social, economic, and political forces within which he lived in the Roman Empire. Paul's hope is tied to his vision of an "earthen vessel" capable of breaking any moment precisely on account of the fact that within it is the treasure of the word of the cross. It is perverse to psychologize Paul's apostolic mission as masochistic escape.[19] The hope of sharing in the glory of God, of being changed from the image of the earthly man to the image of the heavenly (I Cor. 15:49), is not hope that God will eventually do something for mankind. It is hope based on three things that God has already accomplished.

First, that God can actually carry out such a major undertaking is obvious from the fact that he had already done a major undertaking before: he created the world (II Cor. 4:4-6). In the second place, the cross and the resurrection of Christ is a second act of God that has already altered the order of creation in its spiritual, even if not in its material or visible, structures (II Cor. 4:18). In the third place, those who have been called by God to his new creation have received the Spirit as a down payment that guarantees the rest of God's promised redemption (II Cor. 5:5). Waiting for the Parousia the Christian lives in hope, strengthened by the Spirit (Rom. 8:26), walking by faith and not by sight (II Cor. 5:7). But if one grants the reality of a fallen creation "how much more" must one acknowledge the reality of God's act in Jesus Christ (Rom. 5:17).

For Paul this understanding of what had already happened, what was happening by the preaching of the word of the cross, and what was about to happen at the Parousia, had important immediate consequences as to how one had to live while still in this physical body of flesh. The conclusion can be drawn quite readily. "He died for all, that those who live might live no longer for themselves but for him who for their sake died and was raised" (II Cor. 5:15). For the sake of mankind Christ died and was raised; as a consequence those who live in Him must not live the life that He died for them. That those who live might live no longer for themselves could be said also as "that those who live might live no longer in Adam." In other words, "he died for all" in order to destroy the world that we know and live in by ourselves and in order to open up a new possibility for human life.

Not for a moment does Paul doubt that the death of Christ means the end of the fallen creation, but he also knows that the world in which men and women live by nature is still here. That is why Paul describes life while still in the flesh as a life to be lived "as if not in the flesh." It has to be "as if not" because of the tension between the world already destroyed and the world not yet attained. It is because of this eschatological tension that in the Christian life joy and sorrow, pain and comfort are always mixed together (II Cor. 1-6). To live involved in something as if not involved is, to say the least, a confusing doctrine. Does not this argue for some double standard, some hypocrisy, some compromising with the world, some lack of courage, some "occasional conformity" to what is known to be the wrong thing to do?

Paul's instruction to live in the world "as if not" in the world is sandwiched between the following declarations: "But this I say brethren: the time is short . . . for the form of this world passes away" (I Cor. 7:29, 31). In other words, it is clear that Paul's ethical instruction is conditioned by his expectation that the Age of Messiah will any moment now be replaced by the Age to Come. Unlike the passage from this Age to the Age of Messiah which had left no mark in the external, natural world of the flesh, the passage of the Age of Messiah into the Age to Come will bring about a complete and total destruction of "this world." Its "form" or "basic structure" will be destroyed in order to give way for the creation of a totally new reality for those in Christ to live in.

In the meantime, during the "short" time, Christians ought to conduct themselves according to the ethic of "as if not." "Those who have wives be as if they had none, and they that weep as if they wept not, and they that rejoice, as if they rejoiced not, and they that buy as if they possessed not, and they that use this world as if they did not have it" (I Cor. 7:29-31). Certainly what Paul is saying is not that Christians should be unfaithful to their wives, hypocritical as to their true feelings, and liars about their business affairs. Rather, Paul is saying that when the Christian engages in legitimate affairs in the world, because of what he knows about the ultimate destiny of the basic structure of the world, he cannot give any kind of ultimacy to these affairs. Christian life in a world dominated by the forces of sin of necessity results in a tension as to the significance that may be given to a structure which is doomed, and shortly is to be put away definitively. The whole of Paul's advice in these verses and the ones immediately after is conditioned by two considerations: 1) The time is short before the world that we know, and deal with, and organize our lives on, will be totally destroyed by God, and 2) don't complicate life in the world by establishing new social, economic, or political arrangements; these will only diminish the effectiveness of a "co-worker" with God in the bringing about of the final victory by "the Word of the cross."

These same two considerations also inform other well-known words of Paul that have been variously interpreted: "Though I am free from all men I have made myself a servant of all that I may gain the more. And unto the Jews I became as a Jew that I might gain the Jews. To those under the law I became as one under the law . . . that I might win those under the law. To those outside the law I became as one outside the law . . . that I might win those outside the law. To the weak I became weak, that I might win the weak. I have become all things to all men, that I might by all means, save some. I do it all for the sake of the Gospel, that I may share in its blessings" (I Cor. 9:19-23). "For woe unto me if I do not preach the Gospel" (I Cor. 9:16).

In contrast with the "as if not" of Chapter 7 we find here the shorter "as." To the Jew I became *as* a Jew, etc. Paul realized that he could not become a Jew, neither one under the law nor one outside the law. By the grace of God, he was what he was: an apostle and servant of Jesus Christ. He could not become anything else. But for the sake of the Gospel, that is to say, the word of the cross, he became *as* whatever others were in order to save some. In other words, the Gospel had already destroyed some of the distinctions made by the law as to Jews and Gentiles. To have become a Jew or a Gentile would have been to negate the fact that the cross had already put an end to the old world where humanity had been thus divided.

There has been no lack of those who see in these words the evidence for charging Paul with inconsistency in his conduct, at best, or with outright hypocrisy and spiritual pride, at worst.[20] To do this is to fail to realize the apocalyptic framework within which the Apostle understood his whole ministry. Others have tried to defend Paul from these charges only to herald him as the champion of situation ethics.[21] According to them the life of Christians is not governed by absolute rules that are binding at all times but by a love that understands the situations within which they must act and learns from the situation itself the course of action to be followed. Thus, in different situations the same act of a Christian may be both a perfect exemplification or an outright negation of what objective moral standards may demand.

Such a reading of Paul, however, misses the whole point of Paul's remarks. He is not saying that different situations elicit different responses from him because he is always respectful of the other. On the contrary, he is saying that his one concern is to be a minister of the word of the cross, and to carry out to its ultimate fruition what the cross had accomplished is the one and only determinant factor for all his conduct. When Paul says "the love of Christ controls us" (II Cor. 5:14), he is not thinking of love as a force enabling individuals to react responsibly to the demands of changing situations. Rather, he is thinking of the love of Christ as the cross of Christ that has destroyed the world of sin and death. This is an act of God which, however, controls and energized the lives of those who have been reconciled to God by it. Paul would certainly not allow circumstances or situations to determine his actions. He did not relativize what is good and what is evil. He lived under the absolute control that exercised its power over him out of what God had accomplished in the cross of Christ.

As such, the cross of Christ was not a paradigm of human possibilities or of the proper reaction to felt human needs. Neither was it God's participation in human suffering, thus absorbing into Himself the mystery of evil. Rather, it was the divine act that destroyed the world of sin and thus had brought an end to Paul the sinner. The cross and the resurrection were God's act. He had created a new world for men and women to live in and as such had placed all human structures on notice about their temporary nature.

Within this perspective of what was accomplished by the cross of Christ, even the law comes under judgment since it belonged to the age that was destroyed by the death and the resurrection of Jesus Christ. The law had been given to the world of Adam in order to establish the sinfulness of men and women on an objective basis. In as much as the world of Adam continues to exist during the age of Messiah, the law continues to serve as a revealer of sins (Rom. 5:20; Gal. 3:19) and as an enticer to sinning (Rom. 7:7-11). But the cross of Christ has put an end to the world of Adam. The world of sinners has been destroyed by the power of God revealed in the Gospel. Thus, for those who no longer live in the world of Adam, life and conduct is not controlled by the law but by the power of the word of the cross. This does not mean that one who has died to the world of Adam and has been made alive in the world of Christ no longer does things that are incongruous to life in Christ. Indeed, that is the case even for those who are in Christ but still in the flesh. Paul recognizes that and has some specific advice as to how the Christian community is to deal with the sinful acts of one of its members. In the world of Christ the sin of a Christian gives the members of the Christian community an opportunity to "fulfill the law of Christ." He says, "Brethren, if a man is overtaken in any trespass, you who are spiritual should restore him in a spirit of gentleness. Look to yourself, lest you too be tempted. Bear one another's burdens, and so fulfill the law of Christ" (Gal. 6:12). Fulfillment of the law here means something completely different from what it means in the world of Adam. There to fulfill the law meant making sure that not one of the commandments of the law was disobeyed. Here it means in love to uplift the fallen and to restore him or her within "the household of faith" (Gal. 6:10, cf. 5:14).

PAUL AND THE WORLD

It may be an idle exercise to transpose what Paul wrote concerning the cross and the end to the arena of the life of Christians in the Roman Empire, but it may also be enlightening. In any attempt to do this the first question that comes up is how to resolve the tension that characterizes life when conceived apocalyptically. To phrase the question differently, was Paul this-worldly, or other-worldly? Does apocalypticism represent an escape from the harshness of life in this world? Does Paul place so much value in a life outside the world that this life here and now loses all significance? Did Paul pass through this life, travelling extensively in the culturally charged Roman Empire, *as if* he had not been anywhere, all the while living in a portable Christian ghetto?

It is to be kept in mind that for most people of the first century "this world" did not mean the natural world which most moderns consider to be the only real world. For them the world included the supernatural powers designated as angels, thrones, dominions, star spirits, rulers of the world, and the spheres of existence controlled by these powers. Paul himself reports to have been in the third heaven (II Cor. 12:2), and it is clear that he never doubted the existence of supernatural powers who in opposition to God's will controlled human affairs. Middle Platonism in the first century and Neo-Platonism later, under the influence of Roman Stoicism, worked out ways of integrating the divine and the human into a coherent universal structure. What this means is that Paul did not face the choice between this world and another world. Neither Jewish nor Christian apocalypticsm spoke with one voice. As a religious outlook, apocalypticism crossed many frontiers and offered many options. It is not at all certain, for example, that Paul would have agreed with the Book of Revelation's description of the descent of the New Jerusalem from heaven after Satan had fulfilled a one thousand year prison term (Rev. 20:2, 3; 21:2). According to Paul, both those who died in Christ and those who believe in Christ and are alive at the Parousia will "meet the Lord in the air, and so . . . shall always be with the Lord" (I Thess. 4:17). Whether "in the air" means that they shall be in the second, third, seventh, or thirty third heaven is not said. The important thing is that they shall be always with the Lord. In other words, it is not a matter of cosmology but of sociology. The goal is not another world but existence together with the Lord. This is the only passage in his letters where Paul uses the phrase "together with the Lord." Life together with the Lord designates resurrection life, which is achieved and made possible only by the power of God (II Cor. 4:14; 13:4). By contrast life here and now is characterized by its weakness. Paul contrasts not so much two worlds as two forms of existence: one in weakness and one in power. What makes life after the Parousia powerful is that it demonstrates the full power of God in life as men and women live together with the Risen Lord. That is why in this world Christians live waiting not in expectation of the destruction of this world but of the *apocalypsis* of the Lord (I Cor. 1:7).

Basically, Paul is not so much disenchanted with the world as he is held by the power of the Risen Lord and the life that may be lived *in* him now and *with* him later. In the Lord Paul had experienced ecstasy and had spoken in the tongue of angels (I Cor. 14:18f., cp. 13:l). In ecstasy, having lost sense of his body, he had been caught to the third heaven where he "heard most holy words, which humans are forbidden to speak" (I Cor. 12:4, translation mine). Like his Jewish contemporaries, Paul claimed to have had a satisfactory visit to heaven so that he had seen and heard what other mortals must wait until death to see or hear.[22] It is not without significance that his claim to have accomplished a successful trip to the third heaven is presented in the context of the dangers he had faced on earthly journeys. The dangers of life on earth and the dangers facing the ecstatic in heavenly journeys, in Paul's mind, belong together. Somehow the universe is of one piece. But having accomplished this feat, Paul is not engaged in giving out esoteric information about the cosmos or bragging about his prowess in travelling through the heavens. Neither is he anxious to help in bringing about the destruction of this world.

Just as he is not a frustrated Jew who found psychological release from guilt in Christianity, he is not a frustrated human being trying to escape from the world by apocalyptic or mystical means. His ecstatic experiences and his apocalyptic outlook have been interpreted as revealing a social misfit moving about among social outcasts of the Roman Empire. Such interpretation misreads the evidence. It is clear that Paul looked at the world critically. His negative judgment on the world was not expressing his social frustrations. Rather, it was the result of having been gripped by the power of God as demonstrated in the cross and the resurrection and having recognized that full life in the power of God could not be lived in the context of life where other powers also exercise their influence. In the final analysis, Paul's apocalypticism does not represent an escape from the world, its institutions, or its culture, but "the triumph of God over life and thought."[23]

If one wishes to understand Paul's movements in Roman society, it is important to recognize the point that we have been making in the above paragraphs. Through the preaching of the cross, the power of God was being extended over the world and the powers of darkness were being vanquished. Their influence little by little was being diminished. The author of The Acts of the Apostles still has the same vision, even if he has overlooked some of the internal struggles that took place within the movement before the missionary thrust to the Gentiles established itself as the way of the future. It was only later that Christians dropped out of the world, left the cities, and became ascetics in the desert. Paul was neither an ascetic nor an escapist. He took the world as it was and confronted it with the action of God.

CHAPTER V

THE LAW AND SALVATION

Probably no aspect of Paul's thought has been as impervious to explanation as his teaching about the law. Albert Schweitzer, the famous missionary and biblical scholar, came to the conclusion that the only explanation was to admit that in the matter of the law Paul had contradicted himself. Many since have agreed with him. It is not at all difficult to set forth the basic elements of what is taken to be the Pauline inconsistency. Nor is it too difficult to follow the most obvious lines of argument in order to exonerate Paul from it.[1]

PAUL'S INCONSISTENCY ON THE LAW

Paul's ambivalence about the law rests on both his negative and positive evaluation of it. On the one hand, he can say that "the law is holy, and the commandment is holy and just and good" (Rom. 7:14). Or, in a loaded phrase, he can state that the Jews in the law had "the embodiment of knowledge and truth" (Rom. 2:20). If the law is truth that belongs to the spiritual realm, then how can anything wrong be ascribed to it? It would seem that in this light the law is not much different from Jesus who as the Incarnate Son has also been spoken of as the embodiment of truth. As such the law may be properly perceived as a rather invaluable and irreplaceable aid to human salvation. It would seem that Paul recognizes the continuing authority of the law when rhetorically he asks, "Do I say this on human authority? Does not the law say the same?" (I Cor. 9:8). And he seems to link the law to salvation when, personifying the law, he says that "the commandment . . . promised life" (Rom. 7:10). Nothing in the immediate context seems

84

to indicate that it was not within the power of the law to deliver what it promised. Furthermore, on account of the temporary nature of all human arrangements until the imminent Parousia, he said that the presence or the absence of circumcision made no difference but the keeping of the commandments of God did (I Cor. 7:19).

On the other hand, one must read other statements which do not easily fit into the general scheme of things presented above. The tacit assumption that the law could legitimately promise life is challenged by the tacit assumption that it could not. The expression "tacit assumption" is used because it is difficult to argue on the basis of conditional sentences that do not state what is considered to be the actual case.[2] Paul says, "If a law had been given which could make alive, then righteousness would indeed be by the law" (Gal. 3:21b). The argument, it would seem, is that righteousness has never been by law because the law given at Sinai was in fact not capable of giving life, or, as stated here, "making alive."

Over against the notion that the law is basically to be associated with life, or salvation, or the giving of life, there are many more passages where the law is directly linked to sin and death. Rather than to see the law as an agent for salvation, Paul sees the law as an agent of death, basically involved in establishing the sinfulness of all humans and passing judgment on, or condemning, them. The chain that drags men and women into a hopeless death is made of the links "law" and "sin." "The sting of death is sin, and the power of sin is the law" (I Cor. 15:56). In other words, sin is able to kill (sting) people by the power that the law gives it. Other passages elaborate on this sinister connection between the law, sin, and death. In Galatians the apostle makes the half cryptic statement that the law "was added because of transgression" (3:19). This is enough to establish that the law was called for by transgressions, rather than by life. Still it is not clear in what way transgressions call for the coming in, or the adding, of the law.

In Romans, however, Paul elaborates on this theme. There he explains that sin was present in the world before the coming of the law. This, again, points out quite clearly that Paul is not working with a definition of sin as "transgression of the law." Thus the existence of transgressions prior to, and independent from, the law called forth the giving of the law so that sin could now be "counted." In other words, the law identifies transgressions as such and by declaring them to be what they are the law "increased the trespass" (Rom. 5:20). In this way the law aids "sin to reign in death" (Rom. 5:21). As stated in Rom. 4:15, "the law brings (forth God's) wrath."

The difficult question to answer, then, seems to be: Did Paul think that God gave the law at Sinai in order to provide the people with a vision of truth in the spiritual realm? Would it guide them to the promised land and salvation? Or, did Paul think that the law was given by God at Sinai in order to make them realize that by themselves they would forever remain frustrated sinners in a spiritual wilderness.

BASIC CONSIDERATIONS INFORMING THE ISSUE

Before we attempt to give an answer to this question several things should be set forth clearly in terms of the Pauline perspective. In the first place, it must be recognized that we are not involved in reading the mind of God but rather the mind of Paul. God's thoughts or God's intentions are not being examined here. We are not asking: Why did God give the law at Sinai? Rather we are asking: What did Paul think to be the reason for God's giving of the law at Sinai? When the question is understood to be such, it is within the realm of possibility for a writer at different times to give answers that fit the argument which he happens to be constructing at the moment but which fail to be consistent. Thus in searching for an answer to our question ultimate coherence may be neither assumed nor sought.

Secondly, we must be clear as to what Paul meant by law. It used to be fashionable to extricate Paul from the entanglements of his own statements about the law by claiming that Paul made a distinction between the moral and the ceremonial law. This made it possible to relate all the positive statements about the law to the moral law and all the negative statements to the ceremonial law. Even though it is possible to argue that Paul seems at times to have made a distinction between the significance of the moral law of the ten commandments and the laws having to do with sacrifices and social taboos, it has been demonstrated that he does not have this in mind when he uses the word law.[3]

In his thinking about the law Paul shows himself basically as one trained within Judaism.[4] In its immediate context the law is what separates and distinguishes Jews from Gentiles. This is central to Paul because that was the most immediate practical, everyday relevance of the law for the missionary to the Gentiles. The law is what creates and maintains the Jewish way of life. It provides the Jews with the very air they breathe. Because they have the law, they are different.

Throughout the Israelite prophetic period, there had been some tension as to whether it should be understood that the people had been chosen and constituted by God in Abraham, or whether it had been chosen and constituted by God through Moses at Sinai. Thus it has been pointed out that the doctrine of election in the Old Testament has two *points d'apuis*.[5] The same prophet could call attention at one time to one and at another time to the other of these historical moments as the time when Israel was born.

Paul, however, recognized that these two are quite distinct historical moments and that there had been 430 years (Gal. 3:17) separating the two. While Paul looked at the law as the element constituting the people, he is aware that significant historical differences may not be overlooked. Thus he made a distinction between the creation of the people on the basis of a promise to Abraham and the formation of the people on the basis of a law given through Moses. Still circumcision (which was the mark distinguishing the people traditionally associated with Abraham) was considered by Paul, as well as by all Jews, to be the mark of the people who live the Jewish way of life as defined by the law. Throughout the letter to the Galatians, "to desire to be under the law" (Gal.4:21) and "to receive circumcision" (Gal. 5:2) are parallel descriptions of those Gentiles who thought (because "some people" taught them so) that to be heirs of the promise given to Abraham one had to "live as a Jew," as defined by some Jewish-Christian contemporaries of Paul. From all this, then, it is clear that the law had become in its most practical way the means for distinguishing Jews and Gentiles.

The centrality of the law in the Jewish religious consciousness was another very complex rather recent development. Prophetic religion in the Old Testament did demand obedience to God's will and the practical demonstration of obedience in a life of justice and holiness. But it was only after the Exile that, in an effort to reorganize themselves as a commonwealth under God, the Jews codified the Pentateuch and gave it canonical status as the Magna Carta for their political, social, economic, and religious life. After the conquest of Alexander the Great the Jews lived in Palestine as a nation ruled by priests, without political independence until sometime after the Maccabean Wars (167-164 B.C.). With the passage of a few years, however, the actual way in which the Pentateuch had come about was forgotten and the *Torah* (The Constitution) was accepted as of as much authority as the Ten Words which God had given to Moses at the time of the Exodus. Moses was thought to have been the mediator of the whole *Torah*, now understood as having a divine origin. In this way *Torah* in Judaism functioned as that authoritative instruction to be followed in the regulation of Jewish life. The Jewish way of life was not only lived in Palestine where in the fourth century B.C.E. the *Torah* could function as the constitution for society. Jews also lived in every corner of the Mediterranean and Mesopotamian worlds, and it is clear that there also the *Torah* soon became the authoritative scripture guiding one's path in the world. When the Hellenistic cultural invasion spread over the then known world (333-312 B.C.E.) and created peculiar strains in the application of ancient customs within the new social setting, the Jews soon developed ways to adjust the authoritative *Torah* to their new Hellenistic *milieu*.

This process of adjustment, of course, could only be carried out within certain limits, even if those limits varied from one community to another or from one wise man or rabbi to another. Still no Jew could deny the effective validity of the law, either as a way to holiness or as a way to wisdom. To deny it would have been to deny the only means for Jewish self-identity. The *Torah* was what divided humanity into Jews and Gentiles. Thus, for example, Philo of Alexandria, Jesus' and Paul's most famous Jewish contemporary, may have been the object of criticism by some strict rabbis who may not have approved of his attendance at the *gymnasium* or at the entertainment provided by the Roman rulers for the populace of Alexandria. Still he spent his life and energy writing treatise after treatise in order to make sense of the *Torah*, the greatest human expression of divine wisdom.[6]

Paul did not question the divine origin of the *Torah*. He makes, however, a rather cryptic reference to the fact that "it was ordained by angels through an intermediary" (Gal. 3:19). Even if this makes the *Torah* somewhat derivative, it does not challenge the authoritative position occupied by the law. When in his own mind he conceives that some may actually understand that he is doing this, he closes the door to that possible interpretation of his message by writing "Do we then overthrow the law by this faith? By no means! On the contrary, we uphold the law" (Rom. 3:31). For any presentation of the gospel where the righteousness of God is revealed, the Torah is indispensable.[7]

It must be recognized, therefore, that when Paul uses the word law (Greek: *nomos*) he is really thinking of the Hebraic concept of the *Torah*. This is important because the word *Torah* has many connotations besides the legal one. In all cultural traditions there is found the recognition that the laws are the expression of the will of the gods of the land. The famous stone pillar on which the code of Hammurabi was inscribed depicts the king receiving the law from the hand of his god Shemesh. With the advancement of culture and the development of more complex societies the law tends to lose its moorings in the divine will and to become more of an instrument for the human expression of the ideals of justice, impartiality, and equity. In this way the law becomes attached to a legal system. It establishes the legality of a particular case. In Judaism, however, *Torah* retains its character of being that which is taught with authority because of its divine origin.[8] *Torah* was originally the Pentateuch, traditionally associated with Moses and the Exodus. As such it occupied a privileged authoritative position recognized by all branches of the Jewish people before 70 C.E. Yet the Prophets and the Writings, which came from before 70 C.E. were eventually included in *Torah*, while the Mishna and the Talmud, which were written later, were considered as the addition and the completion of the *Torah*. The Hebrew canon made up of its three sections, the law, the prophets, and the writings, could also as a whole be considered *Torah*.

The law represents the expression of God's will for his people which is to be obeyed throughout life, but there was some discussion among Jews as to the possible superiority of some commandments over others.[9] There is no evidence, however, that Paul understood the law in a restricted sense to refer to some portion of it. To him the *Torah* as such comes from God. When he talks of human traditions or human fables or commandments imposed by humans, he is certainly not referring to Pentateuchal legislation, or stories having to do with social or cultic taboos which, even though found in the rolls of *Torah*, are now considered outdated by Hellenistic standards of culture.

In Greco-Roman society the law had been quite secularized. Rome is, after all, the cradle of our Western legal tradition precisely because in Rome the legal system became the arena for the great social struggle of the plebeians against the patrician aristocracy. That formative social experience gave to the law a totally secular face, best depicted by the blindfolded woman with a balance and a sword. Undoubtedly, when the Jews still spoke of their law as a divine oracle that communicated the divine will, Gentiles reacted either with awe or with disdain.

PAUL'S VIEWS ON THE LAW

For Paul, the law participates of a fallen creation. This aspect of Paul's thought is one of the most difficult ones to explain because it is quite foreign to our own ways of thinking. Yet if our aim is to understand the great apostle, we must make an attempt to enter into the view of the world that served as a framework for his theological reflection.

That the creation had "fallen" meant to Paul that the world no longer existed in immediate relationship to God. The Fall indicates that there is a distance between God and his creation. This distance is conceived concretely as a spatial distance which allows for all sorts of "powers," "principalities," "authorities," and "angels" to have territories under their control both in the "heights" and in the "depths" of the universe. These powers control, or at least "mediate," the relationship between God and mortals on earth. Thus even though Paul denies the *real* existence of idols (I Cor. 8:4), he does affirm the existence of "gods" and "lords" in heaven and on earth (I Cor. 8:5). Chief among these "lords" is Satan, who can tempt humans (I Cor. 7:5) to do what they should not and who as the "god of this world" veils the minds of men and women so that when the gospel of Jesus Christ is preached to them they remain unbelievers (II Cor. 4:4). In this way the rulers of the spheres between God and a fallen creation counteract the inherent power always present in the Gospel. On the other hand, to those who have received the power of the Gospel, and are "controlled by the love of Christ" (II Cor. 5:14), none of the rulers of the air the love of Christ" (II Cor. 5:14), none of the rulers of the air can in any way annul the power of Christ's love. Neither "angels, nor principalities, . . . nor anything else in all creation will be able to separate us from the love of God in Christ Jesus our Lord." (Rom. 8:38, 39)

According to Paul, prior to the new creation in Christ (II Cor. 5:17), the whole of humanity existed in slavery to powers called the "elemental spirits of the universe" (Gal. 4:3, 9). It is not easy to determine exactly in what way these spirits are "elemental." In fact some interpreters would deny that Paul is here thinking of "divine beings" or "spirits" at all.[10] It must be recognized that the apostle writing in Greek used only one noun. He wrote of a slavery to the *stoicheia* of the universe. Basically, the word means the essential units that make up more complex structures. Because of their very existence and nature they determine what is possible within the system or larger whole. The Greek noun may be translated by the English noun "elements." Thus it is understood that there are 110 chemical elements. In Greek it was possible to speak of the alphabet as the "elements" of language or of the notes in the musical scale as the "elements" of music. The question is: What did Paul understand to be the elements of the universe to which men and women are enslaved? The clue is given by his description of these enslaving elements as "beings that by nature are no gods" (Gal. 4:8). Thus Paul makes it clear that by *stoicheia* he means elemental beings, or spirits, who determine the kind of existence that mortals may live in a fallen creation, over which they seem to be in control. Notice, moreover, that even though Paul denies that these beings are by nature divine he in no way denies their existence or their power to enslave men and women. In fact, it is to them that he assigns some responsibility for the crucifixion of Jesus (I Cor. 2:8).

The passage in Galatians 4:1-12 also makes clear that bondage to the *stoicheia* was something that both Jews and Gentiles experienced prior to their faith in Jesus Christ. When Paul says "so with us, when we were children, we were slaves to the elemental spirits of the Universe" (4:3), he is talking about himself and all his fellow Jews who lived in bondage even though they knew the true God. But when he says "when you did not know God you were in bondage to beings that by nature are no gods" (4:8), he is referring to the experience of Gentiles. That Gentiles would have been considered by a Jew as slaves to "weak and beggarly elemental spirits" (4:9) does not surprise us in the least. But that Paul would have considered himself and all his fellow Jews as enslaved to elemental spirits, even though worshippers of the true God, may indeed surprise us. In fact, it should not surprise us. The one writing is a Jew who gained a completely different perspective on human existence from his understanding of what God had done in the death and the resurrection of Jesus Christ. As a Christian Paul considers that in a fallen creation all Jews have lived and still live enslaved by the law, if not freed by Christ. It had been the prison house that kept Jews locked in (Gal. 3:23). From a Christian perspective, in its barest forms life under the law as a Jew and life apart from the law as a Gentile were essentially life in bondage to *stoicheia*. Within the fallen creation, as an "element" controlling Jewish life the law had become detached from the being of God himself. When he said that through the law he died to the law so as to live to God (Gal. 2:19), he means that the very Old Testament was the means by which he had understood that God and the law were not one and the same thing and had forced him to make a choice. As a result he had decided to die to one in order to live for the other.

In summary, Paul thinks that the law is characterized by two things: one is its historical character and the other is its belonging to the world of the intermediaries between God and humans. These two characteristics are clearly reflected in the following Pauline words: "Why then the law? It was added because of transgressions, till the offspring would come to whom the promise had been made, and it was ordained by angels through an intermediary" (Gal. 3:19). As the context makes clear, Paul thinks that "the offspring (of Abraham) to whom the promise was made" is Christ rather than Isaac and Jacob and their descendants. Thus the historical period of the law is from 430 years after the giving of the promise to Abraham to the time when the one to whom the promise was made should come, that is, the coming of Christ. That the law was given through an intermediary would seem to be a direct reference to Moses, the lawgiver. But that it was "ordained by angels" is a rather puzzling expression.

Since Paul did not elaborate on his meaning, we can only interpret the phrase in the context of the letter to the Galatians and what it says about the Jewish way of life under the law as

ordained by angels would indicate that the "angels" or "principalities" or "powers" ruling the spheres between heaven and earth had
something to do with the actualization of the law among human
beings. Paul is pointing out that, even if the law is of divine
origin and in harmony with the promise given to Abraham, the law
must take a secondary place because its objectification has made
it capable of being "handled," of being "mediated," and of being an
"element" within the world.[11] By contrast the promise, or the
Gospel, remain forever a power outside the universe bringing about
supernatural effects within the world.

This much, at least, is clear as to how Paul saw the law
and its characteristics. In order to come closer to an answer to
our original question we must explore now what Paul thought had
been the function of the law in the period between Moses and
Christ.

THE LAW'S PRIMARY HISTORICAL FUNCTION

Paul speaks of the law during this period as having applied
only to "us," that is, us Jews. Paul characterizes this period in the
life of the Jewish people as the period of childhood. The metaphor
brings to Paul's mind the type of existence lived by children of an
upper middle-class family of the Hellenistic Age. It would, in fact,
be consistent with what we know of Paul's own social class to
imagine that he is thinking of his own experience as a child.
Unlike the experience of modern children of upper middle-class
families in highly mobile, industrialized societies who receive most
of their childhood training from a non-working mother and an
occasional, irregular babysitter, children of these families in the
Hellenistic Age lived in a world ruled by household personnel. The
parables of Jesus also speak frequently of stewards, managers,
rulers of the household, doorkeepers, etc. In the Roman, Hellenized
Jewish world in which Paul grew up in Tarsus, as well as in the
Roman world at large, most of the household personnel were slaves
who had to conduct themselves according to the household rules
set up by the master of the house. These rules were mostly similar
in all households. Yet it was the privilege of the master to introduce or delete rules and also to establish which rules would be
particularly enforced in his house. One of the things left to the

particularly enforced in his house. One of the things left to the discretion of a household master was to determine the age at which his sons would cease to be responsible to household slaves and become accountable for their conduct directly to himself. Prior to that age the supervision of the activities of a child during his waking hours and the administration of discipline to the child, would be the responsibility of the household slave known as the *paidagogos*, that is, the guide, conductor, or leader of a child. He was not the tutor or teacher of the child. For formal instruction the *paidagogos* would take the child to his teachers and tutors. He was responsible for the safety and the well-being of the child; he supervised his comings and goings, his play and his sleep, to make sure that the child was where he was supposed to be or did only what he was supposed to do. When the child ceased being a child, the first noticeable difference was that he could leave the house and go places unaccompanied by his *paidagogos*. A sign of the father's trust and respect for his child would be to recognize his growing maturity and allow him to go places by himself.

Paul explains that one of the basic functions of the law had been to be the *paidagogos* employed by God to supervise Israel while still a child (Gal. 3:24f.; 4:1-5). As such, the law made sure that Israel did not wander away from the house of God, exposed to the dangers that may overtake children in the world at large. But this confinement to the household could at times seem, from a limited perspective, to be a denial of the rights of children of a free master to be themselves free. Metaphors, however, have a limited range of applicability. The metaphor of the *paidagogos* only tries to say that while children may certainly need a *paidagogos* the services of one are unnecessary once the child has grown to the age stipulated by the father, at which time the child is transferred into an adult world. It would have been considered ridiculous for young adults to walk with their *paidagogos* in tow. Things that are right and proper and according to the will of the father at a particular stage of life may not be so at a later stage. It must be remembered also that the notion of the stages of life was one of the stock notions of the Hellenistic age. It is clear from all this that there was nothing intrinsically wrong with the law nor that God changed his mind about how to deal with mankind because things had worked differently from what He had expected. As Paul sees it, everything was working out according to God's sovereign will and mankind's maturing process.

Besides the law's historical function as the *paidagogos* for Israel's period of childhood, Paul recognizes that the law also serves an important psychological function in the uncovering of sin within the human person. Paul agrees with the notion that sin entered the world through the activity of Adam (Rom. 5:12), but he does not go on to say that all persons are sinners because of Adam's sin. For him the recognition of the entrance of sin in the world is the way of accounting for the entrance of death within God's world. If all humans since Adam have died, it is not because of Adam's sin but because of their own sinning in a world under the power of sin. "Death spread to all men because all men sinned" (Rom. 5:12b). For Paul the connection between sin and death is so obvious that it needs no proof. Thus the sinfulness of all persons is established by the death of all. While persons are alive, it is possible for them to pretend that they are not sinners. In other words, while they live sin may be present in their lives, but since it is not apparently bringing about their deaths its presence may be overlooked or ignored. Sin is personified by Paul as apparently inactive, dormant, "apart from the law sin lies dead" (Rom. 7:8). But it is there all the time, carrying on its deadly work. Humans, however, may live under the deception of thinking that they are sinless since they are alive (Rom. 7:9a). By awakening dormant sin the law brings about an internal struggle.

THE LAW AND CHRISTIAN EXPERIENCE

For Paul the law serves a most significant function not only by objectifying sinful acts as sinful but also by awakening dormant sin and tempting it into action. Paul deals with this particular function of the law in Romans 7, one of the most famous passages in all of his writings. Its fame is built on an autobiographical interpretation of the text.[12] Supposedly here Paul has opened up his own soul and revealed to his readers his own psychological struggle with the forces of sin in his life. Since Freud provided a model for understanding human psychic dynamics, many interpreters have found in Romans 7 the key with which to unlock Paul's personality. According to this line of interpretation Paul was frustrated by an oversensitive conscience that imposed on him an overbearing load of guilt.[13]

Even when no such diagnosis is made of Paul's past life, most scholars still see in Romans 7 some autobiographical recollections of one who, remembering his pre-Christian past in Judaism, cannot help feeling again the frustration and the pangs of guilt that supposedly are part and parcel of Jewish life under the law. In the words of Beker, "The depth of Paul's description suggests that a Christian interpretation of Jewish existence under the law is the primary subject matter of Romans 7. He describes the schizophrenia of the unredeemed person."[14]

In Chapter 3 above we touched on Romans 7 and established what we consider to be the proper context for the correct under-standing of the passage. Paul is writing eschatologically rather than autobiographically. Even in such a context, however, it may be recognized that the law has a psychological role to play. The law may disturb an otherwise pleasant way of life and make it unbearable, but it may do this without necessarily being of itself unbearable. Let us note that it is precisely in this context that Paul goes out of his way to make clear that there is nothing essentially wrong with the law. Here he proclaims the law to be spiritual, just, good, and holy (Rom. 7:12, 14). Neither is there anything essentially wrong with men and women living a rather pleasant existence that finds goodness, justice, and the highest ideals in the law (Rom. 7:16b: "I agree that the law is good"; 7:18b: "I can will what is right"; 7:22: "I delight in the law of God, in my inmost self"). Certainly one who agrees with, wills to do, and delights in the law of God seems to be alive and well. But this law that "tacitly" promised life (Rom. 7:10) functions to bring about death by awakening dormant sin (Rom. 7:9). Thus the law has served to make it absolutely certain (Rom. 7:13) that there is "dwelling sin" in men and women (Rom. 7:17, 20).

The presence of such a distasteful intruder is not dependent on the law, Nor is it really dependent on one individual ("me"), but rather is a fact of existence in the order of Adam or, as Paul expresses it in this text, a fact of human existence "in the flesh" (Rom. 7:18), or "in a body of death" (Rom. 7:24). As long as life is lived in the order of Adam, the conditions of existence shall con-tinually thwart the best efforts or intentions of men and women. In the order of Adam the law serves to create a psychological battle field between knowledge and will on the one hand, and the actual situation and performance on the other. As Paul makes clear the only way out is not to get rid of the law or to get rid of "myself" but rather to allow God to deliver "me" out of the order of Adam into the order of Christ (Rom. 7:25). But this is not something which God does for one privately. He did it once for all men and women in the cross and the resurrection of Jesus Christ.[15]

Let us notice again, moreover, that this deliverance does not quite completely transpose human existence out of the realm of flesh or Adam. For the moment it has opened up the world of Christ, but it has not eradicated the world of Adam. Having asked, "Who shall deliver me?" Paul answers his own question by exclaiming, "Thanks be to God (who delivers me) through Jesus Christ our Lord" (Rom. 7:24, 25). He then concludes the argument with the words, "Therefore, I myself, on the one hand, serve a law of God in the sphere of the mind, and, on the other, a law of sin in the sphere of the flesh" (Rom. 7:25b, my translation).

By establishing that the same individual operates on two fronts or two spheres at once, Paul is able to confront the problem of Christian life in this world. His is an eschatological solution that sees Christian existence in tension between two possibilities. What is unusual here is that the two realms are set forth as mind and flesh. As we shall see in the next chapter, these are usually presented as flesh and spirit. The intellectualizing twist provided by the word *mind* may have been here dictated by the way in which Paul was arguing about the law as something which must be understood, agreed upon, and willed to act upon.

What is more noteworthy still is that in setting up the two realms in which the same self may act, Paul characterizes the law in one as a "law of God" and the law in the other as a "law of sin." It would seem, therefore, that in as much as persons live in the world of Adam, the law that awakens dormant sin within them and makes sin exceedingly sinful may be described as the law of sin, even if the law as such is not sin (Rom. 7:7). In other words, in the sphere where sinning is the most prevalent activity the law is characterized as "the law of sin." On the other hand, the law that regulates life in the world of Christ is now called "the law of God." In another context Paul calls it "the law of Christ" (Gal. 6:12). Obviously Paul is not specifying a different law. He is rather making clear that the will of God *functions* differently in the world of Adam and in the world of Christ.

If in Romans 7 Paul uses the first person singular it is not because he has turned autobiographically to speak of his own frustrations as a Jew with a hyperactive sense of guilt. Rather it is because he recognizes that the reality of the world of Christ always stands over against the reality of the world of Adam. If there is a difference between Galatians 3, 4, and Romans 7 the difference is that in Galatians Paul argues historically, but in Romans he argues existentially or psychologically. Yet both in Galatians and in Romans Paul recognizes that as objectified in the world of Adam the law has been detached from God himself and, therefore, turns out performing secondary roles not exactly in accordance with its possibilities.

Let us reconsider our earlier question. Did Paul think that God gave the law at Sinai in order to provide the people with a vision of truth in the spiritual realm? Or, did he think that the law was given to make the people realize that by themselves they would forever remain frustrated sinners? On the basis of the above presentation, we see that the question had been poorly phrased. As it stands, the question presupposes that Paul had been a frustrated Jew himself and that he came to blame the law for his frustrations. It has been argued here that Paul was a rather happy Jew who had no particular desire to shed off his Jewish heritage (Rom. 3:14; 11:1, 2; I Cor. 4:4; 15:9; Phil. 3:4-6). As stated, the question also ignores what we have tried to emphasize most about Paul's theological outlook, namely, its apocalyptic framework. As asked the question posed a false alternative. As a matter of fact, the law does express God's will; it is spiritual, that is, it deals with a reality that is not of this world. Paul's use of the Scriptures argues for his understanding of the divine origin and authority of the law (*Torah*). But in as much as it had been objectified in the world of Adam, the law could no longer function as the revelation of God's righteousness for those who live in the new creation in Christ. In the world of Christ, where righteousness is established by faith, "righteousness is manifested apart from the law" (Rom. 3:21). That is why, with a view to the attainment of righteousness on the part of everyone who believes, Christ is the end of the law (Rom. 10:4). In Christ the historical purpose of the law reached its goal.[16] As a means to righteousness, the law's run is over. Christ has taken its place. To desire to use the law in order to establish one's own righteousness (Rom. 10:3) would be anachronistic.

As already argued above, Paul was not an idealist who refused to recognize the fact that mankind still lives in the world of Adam. Even those who through baptism participated in Christ's eschatological creation of a new world still live in tension with the world of Adam where the law continues to fulfill its traditional functions. It is only at the Parousia that the tension will be removed.

OBEDIENCE AND CHRISTIAN EXPERIENCE

While, on the one hand, Paul contrasted the hearing faith and the works of law as the characteristics of living like a Christian and living like a Jew, it must be noticed that he considered obedience to be of the essence in the world of faith. Christ may be the end of the law, but he is certainly not the end of obedience.[17] For Paul, trust and obedience are the best synonyms of faith. When he wished to congratulate the recipients of his letters, he either praised them for their faith or for their obedience (Rom. 1:8; 16:l9; cf. II Cor. 7:15).

For Paul, who said next to nothing about the details of Jesus' life on earth, the significance of Jesus' earthly life had been his obedience. Jesus's life was not important because of what Jesus was in himself but because of what he did for mankind by his obedience to God. This is best expressed in Philippians 2:8, where Jesus is portrayed as the one who is "obedient even unto death." Quoting these words of an early Christian hymn, Paul makes them his own and gives to them, almost, the significance of a Scriptural passage. The text of the hymn is what supports his advice to the Philippians. The significance of Jesus' obedience is also central in Romans. Building up the contrast between Christ and Adam, Christ is majestically portrayed as the obedient one who undid the work of disobedient Adam (Rom. 5:19).

Obedience is the way of life for all human beings. Everyone lives under a master. What is noteworthy is the way in which Paul sets up the alternatives. "Do you not know that if you yield yourselves to any one as obedient slaves, you are slaves of the one whom you obey, either of sin, which leads to death, or of obedience, which leads to righteousness?" (Rom. 6:16). Here the alternatives are either slavery to sin or slavery to obedience. The alternatives represent the two worlds described in the previous chapter of Romans: either Adam, the sinner, or Christ, the obedient one. In the contrast between sin and obedience is reflected the Pauline ability to use obedience as a synonym for faith. Men and women are slaves either of sin or of faith, which agrees with the Pauline definition "that which is not of faith is sin" (Rom. 14:23). It is clear, then, that obedience belongs to the sphere of faith and that there is a marked difference between obedience and "works of law," which definitely belong to the sphere of sin.

That obedience belongs to faith and life, rather than to law, sin, and death is further demonstrated by the phrase "the obedience of faith" (Rom. 1:5; 16:26). Both texts where the phrase is used indicate that Paul's ministry has been ordained by God to bring about obedience, that is, faith, among the Gentiles. It is therefore unfortunate that most modern translations read "obedience to the faith" as if the faith were a set of rules that needs to be obeyed. That is not the way in which the apostle uses the word faith. The genitival construction "obedience of faith" sets the two nouns in apposition, as almost synonymous. In Romans 10 Paul says that faith comes from hearing and then laments that not all hearing produces obedience, again switching the words (Rom. 10:16). Hearing the powerful word of the cross, faith and obedience should follow. His ministry of preaching the Gospel was to "win obedience from the Gentiles by word and deed" (Rom 15:18). To acknowledge the Gospel is to be obedient to it (II Cor. 9:13). It is, therefore, almost impossible for Paul to comprehend how the Galatians, who had had the Gospel effectively proclaimed to them, could later be "hindered from obeying the truth" (Gal. 3:1-3; 5:7) by the preaching of some other apostles. This was especially so because "for those who do not obey the truth, but obey wickedness, there will be wrath and fury . . . both Jew and Gentile" (Rom. 2:8, 9). They are slaves of sin rather than of obedience.

This much is enough to prove that even though salvation is not related to law, because it works primarily toward condemnation and death, it is related to obedience. Of those to whom he preached the Gospel Paul expected that they should "obey the truth" (Gal. 5:7) or, as he said in another connection, that they should "keep the commandments of God" (I Cor. 7:19). It is not clear, however, that "the commandments of God" are synonymous with "the law" since Paul apparently includes words spoken by the earthly Jesus and his own advice among the former (I Cor. 7:10, 12).

THE SALVATION OF HUMANITY

One of the great tragedies in the history of the interpretation of the Scriptures is the way in which the thought of the apostle Paul has been encarcerated by a slogan. There is no question that Paul believed in righteousness by faith rather than by works of law. This for him was an either/or situation and as far as he was concerned only righteousness by faith, or life in the world of faith and Christ, meant salvation. In spite of its enticing, immediate rewards, righteousness by works of law belongs to a world that ends in death. Righteousness by faith, however, is not a slogan for Paul. It is a meaningful descriptive phrase. In much modern theology it has become, unfortunately, a dogma thoroughly intellectualized, knowledge of whose intricacies may be examined in order to test orthodoxy. Even in the letter to the Galatians where Paul argues strenuously in order to defend the "truth of the gospel" (2:5; 2:14; 4:16), he does not identify the truth of the Gospel with right-eousness by faith but rather with the freedom for which Christ made men and women free. That is to say, for Paul what the power of the Gospel has changed is the quality of life made possible by the death and resurrection of Christ.

Paul uses many metaphors in order to elucidate what salvation is about. These metaphors come from different aspects of everyday life. All of them speak to the reality of salvation; none of them may be safely absolutized or systematized into a theological con-struct.[18] Metaphors were never intended by Paul as building blocks for his theological edifice. Both ancient and modern theologians may use justification, sanctification, and glorification as three different stages in the process of bringing a sinner to be one with God. But that is not the way in which Paul used these words. To him they are helpful metaphors to describe one and the same thing.

The other Hellenistic Jew whom we know well, Philo of Alexandria, did think of the process of attaining to a vision of God as a struggle with the world of sense in which at different stages one achieves certain *plateaux*, each one higher than the previous one, which as a group make up the stages in the road from vice to virtue. This was the way in which Hellenistic moralists, mainly the Stoics, understood the good life that ended in some form of transcendence from the earthly realm.[19] This stoic theme persisted in the NeoPlatonists and through St. Augustine entered the main stream of Christian thought.

But Paul clearly differed from Philo and the Stoics.[20] For him salvation is not reached through the attainment of ever higher stages of perfection in the path toward virtue and the Good. Paul understood what Jesus had meant by the Kingdom of God. Salvation is the work of God, which He accomplishes by the establishment of His kingdom. Salvation, therefore, is identified as life in the Spirit, or life in Christ, in obedience or service to God. By contrast those who do not participate in the life of the Spirit "shall not inherit the kingdom of God" (Gal. 5:21). In this sense salvation is not an individual process. It has been accomplished for everyone in one magnificent divine achievement. Salvation is the new existence in Christ in which all the ones baptized into his death and resurrection participate. They constitute the "household of faith" (Gal.6:10). They are the "saints." For Paul salvation is inextricably linked to Christ and his work. In it Christ alone plays the decisive role. The "obedience of faith" is only possible among those who have been transferred by Christ to the world which he himself created for men and women.

Metaphors like reconciliation, redemption, sanctification, justification, glorification, look at salvation from the perspective of family relations, slavery, the sacred/profane dichotomy, legal arrangements, or aesthetic values. Reconciliation points out that two persons who had been friends or relatives, but who had been drawn apart by some obstacle, have now been brought together again into harmony of feeling and action. Redemption declares that those one who had fallen into slavery and had a price on their heads are now free because their ransom has been paid. Sanctification proclaims that the believer has been set apart from the world and now lives in the realm of the holy where God himself dwells. Justification declares that the ones who stood condemned by the law now stand exonerated from the charges against them. Glorification refers to the new value present in those who belong to the new creation, which they received at the same time when they were justified. Paul says, "And those whom he justified he also glorified" (Rom. 8:30c). That the metaphors may be used interchangeably is clear from a text like I Cor. l:30, "He (God) is the source of your life in Christ Jesus, whom God made our wisdom, our righteousness and sanctification and redemption." The four nouns are not intended to show a progressive series. They are just piled on top of each other to refer to the same thing: God as the source of life and salvation.

Basically, salvation is life rather than death. Metaphors are used only to throw light into the quality of that life which is salvation. The moment the metaphors are pressed too hard in order to extract more theological content, above and beyond their intended metaphorical value, they break down. If one takes the metaphor "redemption" and starts asking who paid the price? to whom? it does not take long to be caught in absurdity. Can it be seriously said that God paid Satan the price for the redemption of mankind? Paul certainly used the metaphor but did not say that. If one takes the metaphor "justification" and starts asking, can the sinner be declared righteous by *fiat*? Is that justice? One may end justifying God only by means of "a legal fiction." Justification was not used by Paul as a way of depicting God's *modus operandus*.

The preponderant role of the law in Judaism certainly had a great deal to do with Paul's predilection for the forensic metaphor, but this should not blind us to the fact that Paul is concerned with salvation, life in Christ. Justification is just a metaphor for it. It should not be used as the key that unlocks the door that allows one to enter and watch the way heaven actually operates.

What the apostle envisions for himself and all believers is salvation. That is the ultimate, most comprehensive, description of what life in Christ means. Paul is aware that whereas justification, sanctification, the reception of the Spirit, the power of the preaching of the Gospel were in some measure ascertainable realities in the experience of Christian believers, salvation in its ultimate expression was still beyond them. Arguing from a minor to a major order he says "Since, therefore, we are now justified by his blood, much more shall we be saved by him from the wrath of God" (Rom. 5:9). Justification is known now, but salvation from God's wrath is what ultimately counts.

Even if salvation from a world in which sinning goes on is still in the future, Paul recognizes that in many ways the believer is already saved. Salvation does have specificity now. It is not just a nebulous concept of life beyond. On the negative side, it is said that those saved no longer live under, or in, certain conditions. Christians have been saved *from* the law and its power to condemn. They have been saved *from* the power of the principalities, lords, angels, *stoicheia* who rule over the world of Adam. They are saved *from* the power of sin, and, therefore, ultimately, *from* the power of death.

On the positive side, salvation from sin and death means sanctification and life (Rom. 6:22). As life on earth now salvation is given specificity as freedom (II Cor. 3:17). Salvation and freedom are synonymous. As noted in our analysis of the letter to the Romans, freedom is the theme of chapters 6,7 and 8. Repeatedly, Paul talks about freedom from sin (Rom. 6:22) and freedom from the law (Rom. 7:6). As he sees it ultimate freedom from death not only has to do with humans but also with the whole of creation which "will be set free from its bondage to decay and obtain the glorious liberty of the children of God" (Rom. 8:21). This again sets the tension that marks the existence of the children of God,[21] who, on the one hand, have experienced salvation but, on the other, still groan inwardly "waiting for the redemption of their bodies." Thus the salvation of the children of God, which is an accomplished fact, also includes the hope of the freedom from the decay experienced by everything that still lives in a fallen creation. In this hope the children of God must patiently wait (Rom. 8:23-25; Gal. 5:15).

CHAPTER VI

THE BODY AND THE MIND

Years ago it was not uncommon to read biblical material as if the authors had been Platonists who believed in the soul as a superior, eternal, in fact, the only real, part of a human being that happened for a while to be using a mortal body. This body, then, functioned as a prison for the soul which will achieve its freedom when at death it is able to escape from the limitations that the body had imposed on it.

Besides the body-soul dichotomy and its Platonic understanding of the soul's immortality,[1] a different dichotomy was set up in the nineteenth century under the influence of German romantic idealism.[2] This was the dichotomy of the body and the spirit. According to it, the spirit is given all the genius of individuality and creativity as well as the ability to transcend the separations created by bodies. The spirit can conceive the essential union of all things in nature on account of its capacity to soar beyond the directly observable and, from a higher perspective, enlighten the human understanding of things.

Neither of these views is traceable in Paul, nor does he see human life as a dichotomy. (Or, as sometimes presented, as a trinity of body, soul and spirit.) Modern scholarship has gone a long way in the right track by recognizing the holistic view of human existence present in Paul and most biblical writers. His emphasis on the integrity of the person as body, soul and spirit (I Thess. 5:23) points out that men and women are not made up of parts that have been put together. Essentially, as beings in the world, each one of them is a whole.

PAUL'S ANTHROPOLOGICAL TERMINOLOGY

When considering Paul's thought, the different anthropological terms have to be recognized not so much as designating different parts of the whole person but rather as referring to the whole viewed from a particular perspective or involved in performing a particular function. Thus, even if there are disagreements among scholars as to which concrete aspect of the whole a particular word points out, by and large it is agreed that Paul had a holistic view of human nature.[3]

The key anthropological terms used to designate the characteristics of human existence and activity are the words *flesh, spirit, soul, heart, body, mind, and man* (*anthropos*). To be brief, it could be said that *flesh* emphasizes the fact that men and women live in an ecological system in which sin and death are part of the life cycle. As such, flesh is, by comparison, a weak environment. That is why death has been able to reign in it. Basically, flesh is the "natural" way of life for a fallen creation. By contrast, *spirit* is strong; it is able to rule over and destroy flesh, impose its own presence, and work as a substitute for flesh. Thus spirit provides an alternative to flesh as an environment in which human life may take place. Whereas flesh is natural, spirit is from God and identifiable with Christ, who is also from God. Thus to be "in the Spirit" or "in Christ" is actually the same; both expressions speak to the fact that Christians live by, or under, God's power. As power, the Spirit brings about the resurrection of Christ and that of all those who believe in Him who raised Jesus from the dead (Rom. 8:11; 15:13; 15:18f.; I Cor. 2:3-5; I Thess. 1:5f.). As the endowment of a new creation, the Spirit certifies the effectiveness of Christ's resurrection in human life and transfers the believer to his own realm (Rom. 5:5; I Cor. 2:12; 6:19; II Cor. 1:22; 5:5; 11:4; Gal. 3:2, 5, 14; 4:6; I Thess. 4:8). Besides these functions, the Spirit also guides the lives of Christians as the director, or conductor, of life (Rom. 7:6; 8:2; II Cor. 3:6; Gal. 5:13-16). In this way, in the new aeon the Spirit takes the place occupied by the law in the old.

Soul is a word rarely used by Paul. Still his usage is clearly determined by the Hebraic description that when God breathed into the clay-form he had molded the thing became a "living soul" (Gen. 2:7). Soul, thus, designates the kind of life peculiar to Adam and all his descendants. Basically, it is a life that is fragile, capable of being extinguished by a small accident. Men and women who live in the creation of which Adam was the first live a "soul-life" (I Cor. 15:44f.). It is important, therefore, for Paul to stress that the life that those in Christ will have after the resurrection is not going to be a "soul-life." That life will have a different point of departure and, therefore, a different constitution. It is not going to be fragile, mortal, corruptible, but rather strong, immortal, and incorruptible. In as much as they are souls, humans are mortals. By extension, as in common usage, soul may be used to designate individuals, as when the apostle says that "there will be tribulation and distress for every human being (soul) who does evil, the Jew first and also the Greek" (Rom. 2:9). Here as in many other passages, the translators accurately render soul as human being.

In his usage of the word *heart*, again, Paul follows Hebraic usage. To have heart is to have the ability to decide for a particular course of action. Therefore, he who wishes to influence the will of others must win their hearts. The heart is not primarily the center of a person's emotional life but that of his will. It is recognized, of course, that in the exercise of the will everything a person is enters into the decision-making process, including the emotions, the desires, the ability to reason, and the hidden secrets of the heart (I Cor. 14:25).[4] Since we consider the will to be a mental faculty by means of which humans are able to transcend instinct, it should not surprise us to find that Paul assigns to the heart what we would consider functions of the mind. This may have been due in part to Stoic terminology familiar to Paul. The Stoics divided the soul into the rational and the irrational and described the ethical task as consisting in training the rational soul to control the irrational. Most Stoic teachers located the rational soul in the heart.[5]

From among the anthropological terms listed above, the one which received a most markedly Pauline imprint was the term *body*, as has been noted by most Pauline interpreters. Peculiar to the word body, when seen within this context, is that the Hebrew language did not have an equivalent. This means that when the Greek translations of the Hebrew Old Testament used the word body, more often than not the original Hebrew word was flesh, meaning the material structure of muscles, bones, organs and skin in which human life is lived. We have had occasion already to remark about the lack of abstract concepts in classical Hebrew.

The notion body, after all, also belongs in this category even if sometimes it is not recognized. A body is certainly not the sum of its members. In order for the members to be a body, they must be organically joined together so that they are all nourished and able to grow together (Col. 2:18). The whole is certainly more than the sum of its parts. Paul's usage of the word body builds on the abstract quality of the concept.

THE BODIES AS CONDITIONS OF SOCIAL EXISTENCE

Paul used the word body to speak of three different kinds of human existence. As far as he could see, life without a body could not be an active life, capable of expressing itself meaningfully in human relationships. Thus, a disembodied life, even if contemplated as possible, represents no attractive option. "Naked" existence (II Cor. 5:3) is not what Paul looks forward to.[6] What he desired was to be clothed with the glorious resurrection body (II Cor. 5:4). Disembodied waiting for the resurrection is no active life but like a sleep, a dormant state of waiting in Christ. And if in his last years Paul seems more eager to "depart and be with the Lord" (Phil. 1:23), he is hard pressed to make up his mind. The advantages of that option, "being with the Lord," are neutralized by the fact that "naked" he would not be able to do what he does when he lives in his body, namely, honor Christ (Phil. 1:20). The expression "now as always Christ will be honored in my body whether by life or by death," as the context makes clear, does not say that the apostle expects to honor Christ either while alive or while dead. Rather, contemplating the eminent resolution of his imprisonment either by being released for more years of "fruitful labor" (Phil. 1:22) or by the imposition of the sentence of death, in either case he is of good courage. He hopes not to be put to shame by the way in which he honors Christ in his body by his conduct in a life of further ministry or by his conduct at his execution.

Active life that expresses itself in a meaningful and account-able way, therefore, can only take place in a body (II Cor. 5:10). What is important to notice is that for Paul the term body is *his* word for describing what in previous chapters has been called the world (or sphere) of Adam and the world (or sphere) of Christ. He calls them "the body of sin" (Rom. 6:6) and the "body of Christ"

(Rom. 7:4). This is the Pauline way of expressing the tension of Christian existence. It is the result of having been integrated into the body of Christ without having been released from the "mortal body" (Rom. 6:12). This is the tension which Romans 7 is all about and which finds its climactic expression in the desperate cry "O wretched man that I am, who shall deliver me from the body of this death!" (Rom. 7:24).

Christians still live in mortal bodies, and because they do, their vision may not be as far-reaching as faith could make it. In bodies of flesh people are weak and in continuous contact with sin's activities. They are subject to death. They share in Adam's fallen creation. Because of the weakness inherent in flesh the power of sin finds a lodging in them and is dormant within, ready to kill them as soon as the chance should appear (Rom. 7:8-11). In mortal bodies, in human "members," there are forces at work that aim at destruction (Rom. 7:21, 23). It is in view of this fact, a fact that the Corinthians had forgotten, that Paul counsels them, "Let any one who thinks that he stands take heed lest he fall" (I Cor. 10:12)

The Mortal Body and the Body of the Resurrection

For the Corinthian Christians, who believed that through baptism they had experienced Christ's resurrection, Paul develops a concise argument to disprove their claims. They claimed to be "spirituals" (I Cor. 3:1), "wise" (I Cor. 1:20), and "perfect" (I Cor. 2:6). In fact, as far as they were concerned, they were already living the life of the resurrection, having already transcended the realm of the flesh.[7] Paul, however, denies all that. He insists that he has to talk to them "as men of the flesh," not as perfect or mature but "as babes in Christ" (I Cor. 3:1).

To prove his point, Paul develops a tripartite argument about the resurrection. Step one establishes that there is such a thing as a resurrection from the dead, as a general principle (I Cor. 15:12-19). Its purpose is not to prove that there is a resurrection. The Corinthians believed in the resurrection. In fact, they thought they had already experienced it at baptism. What Paul is proving to them is that the resurrection is *from the dead*. In other words, resurrection does not happen to the living who continue to live in the same bodies they had before. The resurrection of Christ must be affirmed as a resurrection *from the dead*. Otherwise, the reality of the death of Christ could be challenged. To the Corinthians the death of Christ was only a performance where the main actors returned to heaven leaving the empty shell of a body for the Roman soldiers to carry on with the show. From the fact that Christ rose *from the dead*, as the earliest Christian tradition affirms (I Cor. 15:3-5), it must be understood that Christians hope for a resurrection from the dead. Christians don't triumph over death by sidestepping it into a spiritual experience in this life.

The second step in the argument (I Cor. 15:20-34) affirms that there are two resurrections and that the first one only establishes the certainty of the second. Even if the two are separated in time, they both represent the raising of the dead and the ultimate destruction of death itself. Christ as "the first fruits of those who have fallen asleep" does not bring about the immediate resurrection of those who believe in him. They have to wait until the Parousia. So Christian hope is not for a resurrection in this life but for a resurrection *of the dead*--"otherwise, what do people mean by being baptized on behalf of the dead?" (15:29). They do it because of their belief in a future resurrection of those who have died.

The final step in the argument provides the conclusive proof that the Corinthians are in error (I Cor. 15:35-58). The Corinthians had been laughing at the notion that the resurrection involved the dead. Working from the notion that the *real* life did not need a body, they ridiculed the idea of the resurrection of the dead by asking sarcastically, "With what kind of body do they come from the grave?" Here Paul introduces the notion that there are different kinds of bodies. The resurrection of the dead should not be dismissed by ridiculing the body. As a matter of fact, that the Corinthians still live in the body of their "soul-life" proves that they have not yet experienced the resurrection for which Christians hope as their ultimate victory over death. When their "soul-life" is transformed into their "spirit-life," then the Corinthians will have experienced the resurrection. In the meantime, they should quit their foolishness and their high claims to being "perfect," "wise," "spiritual," who "know all things" (I Cor. 8:2). The apostle pleads, "Come to your right mind, and sin no more . . . Therefore, my beloved brethren, be steadfast, immovable, always abounding in the work of the Lord, knowing that in the Lord your labor is not in vain" (I Cor. 15:34, 58).

Because they think that they had experienced the resurrection and that therefore they now "owned everything" (I Cor. 3:21) and "all things were lawful" to them (I Cor. 6:12; 10:23), the Corinthians are reminded that they are still living in their bodies, in the flesh, and that they are accountable before God for the deeds done in the body (II Cor. 5:10). If, as some Corinthians held, they had *already* experienced the final judgment and the resurrection, then "let us eat and drink" and "fighting with beasts at Ephesus" makes no sense at all (I Cor. 15:32). But as a matter of fact, Christians still live in the flesh, in their mortal bodies. The body of the "spirit-life" is not yet theirs. For that one they have to wait until the Parousia (I Cor. 15:23-26; Phil. 3:20f.).

The Body of Christ

While waiting for the Parousia and the reception of the immortal, spiritual body, the Christian is not condemned to live controlled by the limitations and the weaknesses of the body of sin. Baptism has opened up a new way of life. It is not life in the "spirit-body." It is life in the body of Christ (I Cor. 12:13). Living in this fallen world, life in the "spirit body" is not an option but life in the body of Christ is.[8] In Rom. 6-8 the options are clearly set forth. Thus, as the "old man" living in the body of sin has died, the "new man" need no longer be a servant of sin (Rom. 6:2). By means of the body of Christ Christians live no longer to serve sin and law but to serve God (Rom. 7:4). Still Christians live in a body where natural tendencies of the flesh operate and make their participation in the body of Christ somehow precarious. Therefore, together with all creation, Christians also moan and groan while living in the world in a body subject to decay and waiting for "the redemption of the body" (Rom. 8:23). In the meantime, "we are debtors" in that the Spirit gives new life to the mortal body and kills "the deeds of the body" (Rom. 8:12f.).

Life in the Spirit, or by the Spirit, is life in the body of Christ. Each body lives in its own ecological system. The body of sin lives in flesh and according to the flesh. The body of Christ lives in Spirit, and according to the Spirit. Christians by the Spirit put to death the deeds of the body, so as not to live "according to the flesh," and make their bodies become "members" of the body of Christ, now working out deeds that serve to express the life of the larger body (Rom 12:4f.; I Cor. 12:15-18). They glorify God by making His presence and His power manifest in the world (I Cor. 6:19f.).

Concerning the propriety of Christians eating meat that had been offered to an idol, it is clear that Paul's arguments build upon the Christian's participation in the body of Christ. As discussed in the letter to the Corinthians, the question of whether or not to eat food that had been offered to an idol could arise under different circumstances. The Corinthian Christians, confident of the lawfulness of all things to "spirituals," claimed that they could do it under any and all circumstances. In his discussion of the issue Paul makes reference to three.

One scenario is a rather simple one. A Christian at home considers the question, "May I go to buy at the butcher shop that sells the meat of the animals that had been sacrificed at Apollo's or Diana's temple?" This Christian is going to buy the meat and bring it home to cook it and eat it with his family. For him Paul has a rather simple piece of advice: "Eat whatever is sold in the meat market without raising any question on the ground of conscience." For this advice he offers scriptural support. "For the earth is the Lord's and everything in it" (I Cor. 10:25f.).

Scenario number two presents a Christian who receives a dinner invitation from his non-Christian Gentile friend. If the Christian is of a mind to accept the invitation, he may go and eat whatever is presented to him (I Cor. 10:27). Parenthetically, it may be noted that a Jew could not have done so and that Paul's advice does not follow the supposed decree recorded in Acts 15. Paul, rather, insists that "the Kingdom of God" does not mean food and drink but righteousness and peace and joy in the Holy Spirit (Rom. 14:17). He could, therefore, have agreed with the Corinthian claim: "Food is meant for the stomach, and the stomach for food" (I Cor. 6:13). As far as eating was concerned, Christians at home or at a non-Christian's home could with a clear conscience eat food that had been offered to an idol. "Food will not commend us to God, we are no worse off if we do not eat, and no better off if we do" (I Cor. 8:8). Neither is the Christian to be concerned about its having being offered to an idol. Paul also agreed with the Corinthian "spirituals" who claimed to know that idols are nothing and, therefore, could not affect food one way or another (I Cor. 8:4).

But if the non-Christian friend who had invited the Christian to dinner pointed out that the food had been offered to an idol, then other things had to be taken into account. As far as the food was concerned or as far as the Christian in relation to his conscience was concerned, nothing had changed. His conscience was clear about the relationship of food to the Kingdom of God. The situation had changed only in that the conscience of the friend of the Christian was unclear about the propriety of a Christian eating this food. At this point, the freedom of the Christian to eat was being checked not by the conscience of his weak friend but by a higher purpose in a Christian's life: to win as many as possible for the Kingdom of God (I Cor. 14:28-33; I Cor. 9:19-23). In their conduct Christians must at all times honor their Lord.

Notice that this is not a "situation ethic" according to which what a Christian does is determined by the way in which a particular situation presents itself. Rather, this is the ethic of the Kingdom of God. What the Christian does is demanded by the absolute ethic of the Gospel (I Cor. 9:23a), which says that under all circumstances Christians must be extending the benefit of the cross of Christ to the world. What controls the actions of Christians is the love of Christ (II Cor. 5:14) that wishes to use them as "earthen vessels" that carry the "treasure" of God's righteousness to all mankind. A Christian who goes to dinner to the home of a non-Christian friend should not be motivated by the desire to exercise the freedom to eat but by the desire to extend the benefit of Christ's cross to an unbelieving friend.[9]

The third scenario envisioned by Paul is probably the one in which the Corinthian "spirituals" were primarily involved. In this case the meat in question is being eaten neither at the Christian's home nor at the home of an unbelieving friend. In this situation the "spiritual" feels "strong" enough as a "man of knowledge" to go and sit "at table in an idol's temple." (I Cor. 8:10). In other words, this Christian wishes to participate in an idol's festival, having a meal at an idol's temple.[10] The reasoning used by a Christian of Gentile background in order to justify such action may be guessed rather easily. "Why not?" could be asked. "The banquets are joyous occasions, and the idols are nothing to fear. We spirituals have vanquished the so-called gods and lords of this world. At these festivals we enjoy the food and the merriment, and celebrate the triumph of Christ over Creation." "Besides," could have been added, "don't Jewish Christians celebrate Passover, other Jewish feasts, and participate in the evening and morning sacrifices at the temple in Jerusalem?"

Confronted with this scenario, Paul offers strong objections that argue against a Christian's freedom to sit at the table of an idol's temple. In the first place, the so-called gods and lords are real (I Cor. 8:5), and they are present and rule over the proceedings of such feasts. Therefore, to eat there is to eat at the table of demons. Idols may be nothing, but demons are a different matter (I Cor. 10:19f.). Moreover, such festivals are part and parcel of a whole system of idolatry (I Cor. 10:14) and immorality (I Cor. 10:8). Thus while eating may be an activity that is harmless enough by itself, being partners with demons (I Cor. 10:20) cancels our participation as members of the body of Christ.

Thus in the qualified scenario number two the Christian does not eat on account of his desire "to save some." In scenario number three the Christian does not eat because he is a member of the body of Christ. Being a member of Christ's body may not be used as an excuse for "living dangerously," "let any one who thinks that he stands take heed lest he fall" (I Cor. 10:12). In ancient times many Israelites who ate manna and drank water from the rock ended up dead in the wilderness at the hand of the destroyer on account of their idolatry, their immorality, and their dissatisfaction with what God provided for them (I Cor. 10:1-11). So also now many who belong to the body of Christ may be denying their membership in Christ's body and be "guilty of profaning the body and the blood of the Lord" by thinking it possible to eat at the table of the Lord and at the table of demons (I Cor. 10:21). A Christian cannot possibly partake of "two breads" (I Cor. 10:21f.).[11] To the Corinthian "spiritual" who feels able to do it, Paul asks "are you stronger than He?" The way in which one establishes the right to participate at the table of the idol's temple may be related to his/her strength. But participation at the table of the Lord is dependent upon God's strength. Strong "spirituals" cannot establish their right here. Therefore, eating at the Lord's table Christians should examine themselves and judge whether they are not being presumptuous, not "discerning the body" (I Cor. 11:29) to which they belong.[12]

Life in the body of Christ is initiated by baptism (I Cor. 12:13), and is maintained by the Spirit that dwells within the

Christian (Rom. 8:9,11; I Cor. 3:19; II Cor. 1:22). In the body the Christian does not live as one but as many who are one. This body is the new temple of God on earth, where God is worshipped in Spirit (I Cor. 6:19). As members of the body of Christ Christians may not, as if they were just one person, do as they please at a pagan temple and sit at the table to partake in a pagan meal or join themselves to a prostitute (I Cor. 6:15).[13] Two who join them-selves together, as Genesis 2:24 says, become one body (the Hebrew says flesh, as mentioned above). Whoever becomes one body with Christ, and in that way has put to death the body of sin, may not "sin against the body" of Christ (I Cor. 6:18) of which he/she is a member. Neither can one resurrect the body of sin in order to make him/herself belong to another body. The Christian is no longer "his/her own." They have been bought with a price. They belong to the body of Christ. Therefore, in the body they must glorify God, both in their conduct in every-day life and their conduct in church (I Cor. 6:20; 10:31f.). Christians may not forget whose body they are.[14]

RESPONSIBLE CHRISTIAN LIFE

From the above discussion, it is clear that for Paul the concept of the body is what gives him a handle on the question of Christian conduct while waiting for the Parousia. It is to be con-trolled not by the law but by the Spirit that energizes the life of the body of Christ. But what about the bodies in which mortals still live? What is to be done with them?

To this question the apostle offers a rather direct answer: Sacrifice them (Rom. 12:1). The Christian sacrifice, which is holy and acceptable to God, however, does not consist in the denial or the punishment of the body as a means to individual perfection. Christians do not sacrifice their bodies on the altar of asceticism or the altar of the superiority of the soul over the body, or of the spirit over the flesh. They do not give up their bodies in order to boast that they did it (I Cor. 13:3). Their sacrifice is the reasonable worship of God. If Paul's own words about this life are to be a clue as to what that means, it would be clear that he carried "always . . . in the body the death of Jesus . . . so that the life of Jesus may be manifested in our mortal flesh" (II Cor. 4:10f.). It is to be observed that this is one of the few passages in which Paul draws significant theological conclusions from Jesus' earthly life. The purpose for this sacrifice, which involves being afflicted, perplexed, persecuted, struck down, etc. (II Cor. 4:8f.), is not to provide Christians with grounds for boasting. Rather it is, again, to extend the gospel and life in the world (I Cor. 4:12). It is for the sake of the cross of Christ that Paul carries in his body the marks of Jesus (Gal. 6:17). Carrying the cross, or the marks of Jesus in the body always refers to the fact that in his life in society his destiny and that of Jesus while on earth were the same.

The reasonable worship of Christians who present their bodies as a *living* sacrifice results in the ability to discern or determine upon examination what is the good and acceptable and perfect will of God (Rom. 12:2). The Pauline words are such that they merit some consideration: "I appeal to you therefore, brethren, by the mercies of God, to present your bodies as a living sacrifice, holy and acceptable to God, which is your spiritual worship. Do not be conformed to this world but be transformed by the renewal of your mind, that you may prove what is the will of God, what is good and acceptable and perfect."

Paul's usage of the word *mind* here is basically the same as that in Romans 7:25. It refers to the total personality seen in reference to the way in which it may live in society according to God's will. In Romans 12:1f., however, there are some significant differences from Romans 7:25. First, we may note that in Rom. 7:25 the contrast is between *mind* and *flesh*. Flesh has to do more with the possibility and the capacity to sin on the part of human beings. It is to be noted, however, that it is after Paul has exclaimed, "Thanks be to God through Jesus Christ our Lord," that he then adds, "So then, I of myself serve the law of God with my mind, but with my flesh I serve the law of sin." In other words, the eschatological gift of God in Christ is what in some sense creates the tension between the mind and the flesh.

Secondly, it must be seen that in Romans 7:25 Paul is at the core of the body of his letter. He is trying to explain how the presence of a new creation in Christ within the fallen creation makes the presence of sin in life somewhat equivocal. As a result even those who in Christ are free from condemnation and live by the Spirit still cry out "Abba, Abba." Even the whole of creation longs for the release from decay and corruption (Rom. 8:15,21f.). Romans 7 also intensifies the unavoidable fact that to live as a Christian in a fallen creation only heightens one's awareness of the power sin exercises within one's environment.

By contrast, in Roms 12:1f. Paul was making the transition to what may be considered the practical working-out of God's righteousness in the community of believers. Now Paul uses the word *body* rather than flesh, and writes in the plural rather than the singular. This is not the language of "confession." He is speaking to the Christian community trying to live out its faith within society at large. He is making clear that Christian worship is not a private affair carried out in the church but rather a social affair carried out in everyday life. There can be no misunderstanding. Paul is not talking about two parts (body and mind) of a particular individual; he is talking about how the Christian community must live and worship God.

If the church allows its life to be integrated into the patterns of life in the world, it may become an ideological force within the cultural mix of the society in which it lives. But Paul does not conceive the Christian community as an ideological factor in the cultural mix. He thinks of it as a saving agent within a fallen world. He wants the community not to be "conformed" but to be "transformed." Notice that both verbs are passive. Whereas the "conformation" to societal schemes of life is the work of forces within society itself, the "transformation" of life is the work of God's Spirit (cf. II Cor. 3:18). Thus Paul's advice is: Rather than to allow society to shape your life, "Sacrifice your body." Rather than to allow the law to transform you into an oddity within society, "Let God renew your mind and allow you to experience His will."

As envisioned by Paul, Christians ought to live guided by the Spirit that operates a renewal of the mind. This operation allows them to discern the will of God and to sacrifice the body as a "rational" worship or service of God. It is only within this perspective that they will see themselves and their responsibilities as they ought to see them (Rom 12:3f.) and understand themselves to be members of the body of Christ properly endowed by the Spirit to perform the tasks assigned to them by God (Rom. 12:5-8; I Cor. 12:14-27).

Paul expresses the same dichotomy of body and mind and the

spending of the one while the other is being renewed, using a different terminology, in II Corinthians. Speaking of the way in which he spends himself on account of his God-imposed necessity to preach the Gospel to the Gentiles, he summarizes by saying: "For it is all for your sakes, so that as grace extends to more people, it may increase thanksgiving, to the glory of God. So we do not lose heart. Though our outer nature is wasting away, our inner nature is being renewed every day" (II Cor. 4:15f.). The word "nature," which brings with it heavy connotations from the history of theology and philosophy, is not Paul's. He says "the inner" and "the outer man" (*anthropos*). The outer person is to be sacrificed, living one's life in society in the service of the gospel and for the sake of the salvation of some. The inner person is to be continually reinvigorated so that it may guide in the spending of one's life in a way that is according to the good, acceptable, and perfect will of God, making one's living a "reasonable service" to God.

Even though Paul admits that he has spoken in tongues more than any Corinthian "spiritual" (I Cor. 14:18) and that he has had visions and revelations (II Cor. 12:1), including an ecstatic voyage to the third heaven (II Cor. 12:2-4), it cannot be said that his is an emotional religion. Nor can it be said that his conception of the body of Christ is mystical in the sense that it is founded on a vision of things that transcends common experience. Paul does not strive after the loss of bodily sensations in order to achieve the bliss of true love and perfect being in the unity of all being when individuality is lost. Paul is not a mystic. His vision is apocalyptic, and his anthropology is adjusted to account for existence in the body of Christ while Christians continue to live in "this present evil aeon" (Gal. 1:4).

While affirming the reality of a new life in Christ, Paul never forgets that the world in which humans still live is one of "flesh." That is the significance of Romans 7. In Romans 5:12-20 Paul argues for the fact that life and obedience in Christ are more real than death and disobedience in Adam, even though knowledge of the latter seems to be more firmly based on human experience. In Romans 6 Paul contrasts the two possibilities for human existence and explains how baptism accomplishes the transferal from one to the other. Romans 7, then, recognizes that mortals have not yet transcended the world of Adam. Even as the law comes and awakens sin and creates all kinds of covetousness (Rom. 7:5, 8), so also to the ones "discharged from the law" (Rom. 7:6) the coming of Christ into their lives leaves them with a dilemma. With their minds they serve the law of God but with their flesh they serve the law of sin (Rom 7:25). It is to be noted that Paul works with the conditions for human existence set in contrast in Romans 5:12-20. Mortals who still live in the natural world as Christians waiting for the Parousia still find themselves within the tension of the body and the mind, even though they are no longer in bondage to the law. That will remain so until they receive the spiritual body of the resurrection which, as Paul takes pains to emphasize, belongs to a "glory" different from the "glory" of life within a fallen creation (I Cor. 15:40f.). Even within a fallen world the "transformation of the mind" of a Christian by the Spirit means that he has passed from "glory to glory" (Rom. 12:2; II Cor. 3:18). He no longer lives as a Jew in bondage to the law but as a Christian in the "freedom" (bondage) of the Lord Jesus Christ serving "the law of God with my mind" (Rom. 7:25).

Waiting for the Parousia (I Cor. 1:7; Phil. 3:20f.) the Christian lives under the guidance of a "renewed inner man," or "a renewed mind," or "a conscience that bears witness in the Holy Spirit" (Rom. 9:1), or a heart into which God has sent the Spirit of his Son crying "Abba Abba" (Gal. 4:6). Renovated by the presence of the Spirit as a gift of God (Rom. 5:5; I Cor. 2:12; 6:19; II Cor. 1:22; 5:5; 11:4; Gal. 3:2, 5, 14; I Thess. 4:8), the mind or the heart may in confidence live in this world fully persuaded of the course to be followed. To live in this world Christians must use their minds so as not to be deceived (I Cor. 6:9; I Cor. 15:33), either by the powers of this aeon who try to blind them so as "not to see the light of the Gospel" (II Cor. 4:4) or by apostles who may present a gospel different from the one of which Paul is a minister (Gal. 1:9). The integrity of the mind is such that once renewed by the operation of God's new creation in Christ it is to be trusted, and appealed to, as the only court of appeal when matters of conduct are at issue.

With the Corinthians the apostle pleads "judge for yourselves what I say" (I Cor. 10:15), "come to your right mind" (I Cor. 15:34), "Don't be fools" (I Cor. 15:36). Certainly the truth of the gospel is the result of revelation, but when expressed in discourse the revelation must make sense in terms of the believer's experience of the power of the Spirit. The final court of appeal is the guarantee provided by the Spirit or the heart (II Cor. 1:22; 5:5). Thus, the Galatians who ignore the significance of their own reaction to the Spirit are called "morons" by the apostle (Gal. 3:l). Most often his appeals are for a thoughtful consideration of a command of the Lord (I Cor. 9:14), or the Scriptures (I Cor. 9:8), or an early Christian formula of faith (Cor. 15:3-5). But also appeals to logical argumentation (if this is so, how much more . . . Rom. 5:17), or to plain common sense ("I speak as to reasonable people" I Cor. 10:15, "to give a human example" Gal. 3:l5).

The integrity of the minds of Christians is an indication that the spirit dwelling in them argues with them. Thus Paul insists that Christians must do things with "full assurance" (Rom. 14:5). They must be convinced in their own minds.[15] To do something with doubts or with a divided mind is to do it without faith and, therefore, is a sin (Rom. 14:23). For Paul to say that his conscience bears witness with him (Rom. 9:1) is the same as to say that he "knows and is fully persuaded in the Lord Jesus" (Rom. 14:14) of what he is writing about. Individual Christians must act in faith out of a mind that is fully persuaded or, as he says at times, "a heart that believes and lips that confess" (Rom. 10:8-10), again expressing the integrity of the mind and the body.

As a community of believers that is constituted as the body of Christ, the members must at all times protect the integrity of the body, "discerning the body" (I Cor. 11:29). They must also as the body of Christ possess one mind, "the mind of Christ" (I Cor. 2:l6). For Paul the thing that fills his cup of joy is to know that a church thinks with one mind (Phil. 2:2; Rom. 12:16: 15:5; II Cor. l3:11). Thus to his favorite church, the one at Philippi, he counsels, "Let those of us who are mature be thus minded, and if in anything you are otherwise minded, God will reveal that also to you" (Phil 3:l5), presumably so that all may have the unanimity of mind that is concomitant with the unity of the body of Christ.[16]

And what is it that they are to be "thus minded" about? They are to think about themselves soberly, that is to say with a healthy mind, and not think that perfection is a Christian achievement reachable while in this "lowly body." They must have the mind of Christ who, though he actually was one with God on equal terms, humbled and emptied himself to become a man and in obedience died on a cross (Phil. 2:1-8). Having the mind of Christ, therefore,

Christians forget whatever they may be in human society. "Counting everything as worthless" (Phil. 3:7f.), they offer their life in society (their bodies) as a living sacrifice, "sharing in the sufferings and death of Christ" (Phil. 3:10). "Forgetting what lies behind" (Phil. 3:13), they press on in answer to the call from above that God sends in Christ Jesus (Phil. 3:14). Christians wait for "the full power of His resurrection" (Phil. 3:10) when He shall "change our lowly body to be like his glorious body" (Phil. 3:21). Sharing in the mind of Christ while active in human society, they live in the tension between the body of death and the body of Christ, but they shall attain to the body of the "spirit-life" in glory.

CHAPTER VII

THE SPIRIT AND LOVE

The reader who has followed our presentation has become well acquainted with the antitheses that characterize the pauline vocabulary. It has been said that "no significant idea of Paul's theology was formulated without its opposite or, more accurately, none is capable of being stated without one."[1] In that case our presentation of the spirit should be coupled to the flesh, as noted in the previous chapter. On purpose, however, we have chosen to join spirit to love in order to show that besides the antitheses there are also complementarities. The spirit is what makes possible the genuine life of creatures. But life in the realm of the spirit is not only created and supported by the Spirit; it is also led by the Spirit. It is ruled by the Spirit. And in as much as it is such it is the life where love works itself out (Rom. 5:5).

In the Hebrew language the word "spirit" has an astonishingly rich range of meaning and to some degree the same is true in Greek.[2] From its basic notion of air in motion it goes on to mean wind, breath, breath of life, person (or individual life), kind of person or personality trait, that which sets the direction of a person's life, or the driving force toward personal goals. It may even point to the all encompassing sense of vitality and drive which mysteriously seems even to play tricks on people who do not recognize the "spirit" that motivates them. The Gospel of John makes a pun on the double meaning of the word *pneuma* in Greek—being born of the Spirit and being born of the *wind* are comparable in that, within the limitations of scientific knowledge in the first century, people knew neither from where the wind or the Spirit came from.[3] *Pneuma* means either one, or both, of them.

Essential to the way in which Paul sees things is that human beings are made up of flesh and live in the realm of flesh. Said in another way, man is by nature a soul (*psyche*). The creation within which Adam was the first brought about living souls (I Cor. 15:45, cf. Gen. 2:7). Men and women do have spirits, but within the Adamic world their lives are not determined by the drives of the spirit but rather by the drives of the flesh. Since the drives of the flesh are constitutionally at war with the drives of the spirit, people find themselves doing something other than what they themselves may have wished to do. (Gal. 5:17).[4] It is within this context, then, that we may understand the Pauline ethic of love as the ethic of the Spirit. The faith that works itself out in love (Gal. 5:6) is none other than the faith that waits in the spirit for the hope of righteousness (Gal.5:5).

LIFE IN THE SPIRIT

Paul, therefore, contrasts quite sharply what men and women can do when they live out of the resources of the flesh, and what they can do when they have access to the resources and live according to the standards of the spirit. The difference between these two modes of life is the difference between life and death (Rom. 8:6, 13). There is an immediate relationship between the conditions under which life is lived and the ultimate outcome of human existence. But life, salvation, is not the goal reached for having lived in terms of higher or better cultural values or having achieved a higher vision of the divine being. As understood by Paul the spirit that is opposed to the flesh is not a more refined taste or a higher religious sensibility. For him it is a question of a life sustained and controlled by the possibilities to be found within nature over against a life that is sustained and controlled by a power that transcends the realm of creation and has been received from the Creator himself.

The modern ethicist who wishes to determine whether Paul was "worldly" or "other-worldly" has a difficult task at hand.[5] Paul is a realist who takes seriously all the difficulties posed by life in this "present evil age" (Gal. 1:4). He never minimizes, or dismisses as irrelevant, the tensions that are inevitable for those who serve the Lord Jesus Christ in a world where sin reigns. On the other hand, he is never able to take seriously the world of flesh, the world of Adam, as the totality of human possibilities. He thinks in terms of the basic conviction that the structure of this

world is to collapse any moment soon (I Cor. 7:29, 31). It was not
within his horizon, therefore, to describe how by efforts of love
and justice Christians could hope to build a better world for their
children.[6] His hope for the future was the "hope of righteousness,"
that is, the hope that God would indeed fulfill his promise and bring
about life and peace on earth by the complete eradication of the
world of flesh and sin. In the meantime, Christians wait not "in
the flesh" but "in the spirit." In fact they "abound in hope by the
power of the Holy Spirit" (Rom. 15:13). The basic test of anyone's
claim to being a Christian is: Do you live in the spirit? What
interests him is whether or not one's life is grounded on God and
His activity or on one's own human endeavors. The Christian life
begins with the reception of the Spirit, which means that Christians
now not only have a new driving force within but also a new
environment about them. Their vision, the panorama within which
they conducts their lives, is one provided by God. The Spirit is a
different sap and a different ecological habitat that allows the
Christian to produce different fruits and reach a different end
(Gal. 6:8). For the Christian, ethical discernment is to analyze the
questions and problems of every-day life from the perspective of
the power of the Spirit Who raised Jesus from the dead.[7] This
Pauline perspective in no way denies to the Spirit the power to
guide Christians in the accomplishment of even radical changes
within the societies where they live.

Paul does not make technical distinctions among different
spirits. Life in the spirit may be guided by the spirit of God, the
spirit of Christ, and the Holy Spirit. He may use all these expressions quite indifferently (Rom. 8:9, 14:17). In terms of what has been
accomplished by God for Christians through Christ, Paul insists
that everything done in this divine operation on behalf of mankind
is the work of God (II Cor. 5:5), who accomplishes everything by
means of *one and the same* Spirit (I Cor. 12:8-11, Rom. 8:11). It is
important to emphasize this monopneumatism in the divine activity.
Paul certainly recognizes the existence of many spirits who can
activate and control human life. The world in which he lived was
full of supernatural powers accomplishing different ends for and
against men and women. For Paul it is important to make clear
that God's action in and through the Spirit is not God acting
through various and sundry intermediaries, each one in charge of
a particular task. All tasks, all ministrations, accomplished by God

are the work of one and the same Spirit, no matter how He is designated. Thus, the unity of the church is not the result of good administrative procedures, successful negotiations in an effort to formulate acceptable credal formulas, or adequate public relations techniques on the part of its leaders. Rather it is the natural outcome of the unity of the Spirit, Who is constantly working toward the building up of the church (I Cor. 14:12).

Besides the unity of the Spirit Paul emphasizes that the Spirit is a gift (Rom. 5:5; 8:15, 23; I Cor 6:19; II Cor. 1:22; 5:5; Gal. 3:2, 5). Paul's terminology on this point is somewhat misleading. Repeatedly he speaks of those who believe in Christ as those who have received the Spirit. This language could lead one to think that believers are in possession of the Spirit, but one should guard against such a conclusion. Paul's language also makes clear that reception of the Spirit does not mean possession of, or control over, the Spirit. The way in which Paul places the declaration "we live in the Spirit" in tension with the exhortation "let us walk in the Spirit" (Gal. 5:25) leaves no doubt. Nothing is to be taken for granted by anyone who has received the Spirit.[8]

The reception of the Spirit makes it possible for men and women to live in the Spirit, but life in the Spirit must also be "led by the Spirit" (Rom. 8:14, Gal. 5:25). In other words, reception of the Spirit does not make one the possessor of the Spirit but rather makes it possible for one to be possessed by the Spirit. It is in this aspect of the activity of the Spirit, as the Possessor, as the Leader, that Paul finds the one characteristic of the Christian life that is most meaningful to him, namely, freedom. As he says: "If you are led by the Spirit, you are not under law" (Gal. 5:18). In Exodus 34:34 Moses, after being with God at the top of Mt. Sinai, was forced to wear a veil so as not to blind the people; but he took the veil off when he came back into the presence of the Lord. Paul deduces from this story that Christians who live continually in the Spirit may be continually unveiled, that is to say, free (II Cor. 3:12-17).[9] Christians who have direct access to God in the Spirit enjoy the freedom that is characteristic of the presence of God while engaged in their earthly activities. Thus life in the Spirit, and led by the Spirit, releases the Christian from the control of external powers and establishes a new guidance system that competes with the natural wishes the person may have or the external constraints of the law as such. That is why reception of the Spirit is not enough. Freedom is found only in being under the lordship of the Spirit. Only those who "are led by the Spirit of God are sons of God" (Rom. 8:14). Therefore, the lordship of the Spirit is not bondage but sonship (Rom. 8:15), by which Paul does not mean the status of minors who are under tutors and custodians but that of adults with full rights to the inheritance and freedom of action (Gal. 4:17, cf. Rom. 8:15).[10]

Action under the leadership of the Spirit could also be described as life under "the law of the Spirit." As Paul says, "the law of the Spirit of life set me free from the law of sin and death" (Rom. 8:2). Here the law of the Spirit is contrasted with the law of sin, and while existence under the rule of one issues in life, the rule of the other results in death. Thus the control of the Spirit that leads to life releases the Christian from the control of the law that could only define sins and condemn mankind to death.

Besides providing guidance for life, the Spirit, being in its very essence power, can do many things which the law given to objectify transgressions could not do. As an energizer the Spirit can produce the desired results. Most importantly, the Spirit not only provides the law but it also provides the new environment where this law obtains. As the law of sin operates in the realm of flesh and participates of the weakness of the flesh (Rom. 8:3), the law of the Spirit also finds it easy to express itself in its own habitat. It was precisely in order to institute this new possibility that God sent his Son "to condemn sin in the flesh," something which the law obviously could not do. If the sending of the Son and his death meant the condemnation of sin in the flesh, the resurrection of the Son meant the new rule of the Spirit, who had raised the Son from death. As a consequence the power of the Spirit brings about not only freedom but also hope (Rom. 15:13). These two make it possible to describe the Christian life as a continuous transformation from glory to glory (II Cor. 3:18). The Spirit of the Lord transforms life from glory to glory in that Christians who through baptism die to the flesh and begin to serve God in the "newness of the Spirit" (Rom. 7:6) receive also an endowment of the very Spirit that raised Jesus from the dead. He who raised Jesus from the dead and gives believers the Spirit at their baptism "will give life to your mortal bodies also through his Spirit which dwells in you" (Rom. 8:11). Life in the Spirit is thus depicted as beginning and ending by an enlivenment that transforms from glory to glory. Paul thought of Christians who live by the Spirit in eschatological terms as a kind of resurrection. This may have been responsible for the fact that both in his letters to the Corinthians and to the Philippians he had to deal with people who understood him to have said that they were already enjoying the glories of the resurrection on account of their having been baptized.[11]

In as much as Christians have received the Spirit, their life now participates of the new eschatological reality created by the resurrection of Jesus from the dead (Gal. 2:16, 20; 3:1-5). For Paul this is of momentous significance.[12] It makes it possible to base his Gospel on the power of God at work for the salvation of mankind, not on some vision which he may have been blessed with and which on account of real or imaginary extraordinary powers of persuasion he may have been able to convince others to accept. In fact, he emphatically denies this latter to have been the case. To the Thessalonians he says, "Our Gospel came to you not only in word, but also in power and in the Holy Spirit and with full conviction" (I Thess. 1:5). He also reminded the Corinthians that his preaching had not been characterized by enticing words but by powerful demonstrations of the Spirit (I Cor. 2:4). These demonstrations of the Spirit were not things that Paul's listeners had seen in Paul. Rather Paul's preaching had been characterized by demonstrations of the Spirit's power in the lives of his listeners. On that account Paul could always point to the effectiveness of the power of the Gospel by appealing to the experience of his converts. The presence of the Spirit in their lives was something they could not deny and he could count on as the ultimate court of appeal whenever his apostleship or his gospel were challenged. He did not need letters signed by the Jerusalem apostles testifying to his apostolic status. His converts were his ministerial credentials (II Cor. 3:2, 3). His ministry was a ministry in the Spirit and under the lordship of the Spirit and therefore a ministry of life and freedom (II Cor. 3:8).

For their eschatological life believers received "the first fruits of the Spirit" (Rom. 8:23). The metaphor is used by Paul in marked contrast with the way it is used in the Old Testament. There it was specified that the first fruits of the harvest were to be brought to the temple and waved before the altar in thanksgiving to God

(Deut. 26:1-11). The offering also served to guarantee a good harvest season. The people were the ones who offered the first fruits to God. Paul, however, reverses the situation. The first fruits of the Spirit are the gift of God to the people. In the strictest sense, God's first fruits is Christ in his resurrection (I Cor. 15:23), but when believers participate in that resurrection through baptism, the power of Christ's resurrection is now operative in their lives as the first fruits of the Spirit (Rom. 8:23). The metaphor of the first fruits is, of course, a harvest metaphor, and the harvest is the basic metaphor for the resurrection. Thus, God's granting to men and women of the first fruits of the harvest is a way of guaranteeing a successful harvest season at the *eschaton*. It should not surprise us, therefore, to see that Paul can also speak of this empowerment of the life by the Spirit at baptism as a "guarantee," or a "warrantee," given believers to assure them of the certainty of the abundant harvest (II Cor. 1:22; 5:5). In other words, the initial empowerment of the Spirit makes the Spirit "dwell" in believers and guarantees that they can continue to live in the world of flesh and still experience full salvation by God's hand at the final resurrection of the dead. That is why the Spirit makes the believer "abound in hope" (Rom. 15:13). The first fruits of the Spirit are the foundation of the Christian life and the grounds for hope.

THE GIFTS AND THE FRUIT OF THE SPIRIT

In the specifics of Christian action in the life empowered by the Spirit, Paul speaks of the gifts of the Spirit and the fruit of the Spirit. The gifts are mainly for the harmonious development of the Christian community as a body. They give to each member of the church a specific function to perform in relation to the life of the whole church. In explicating the gifts of the Spirit, Paul's main objective is to make clear that they may not be used to rate the importance or the authenticity of individual church members. If different members have different gifts and, therefore, perform different functions this does not mean that some members have achieved higher than others and that therefore all church members should strive to achieve what some members have achieved already. Rather the different gifts only emphasize the mutual dependence of church members on each other and their need to coordinate their efforts in order to achieve, not as individuals but as a body empowered by one and the same Spirit, the desired common objective (I Cor. 12:8-13). As a corollary to this, Paul points out that any individual member exercising a spiritual gift should not do it for selfish reasons but should only do it for the building up of the church (I Cor. 14:4, 5, 12, 17, 26).

To the Corinthian enthusiasts who have strong tendencies toward spiritual frenzy, put a premium on the gift of tongues, and seem to feel free to live in a rather promiscuous manner, Paul offers a strong word of advice. They were proclaiming, "All things are lawful for me." In this way they were expressing their freedom to act in a manner that was not in accordance with the law of the Spirit of Christ. Paul agrees with them but gives their slogan its correct context; he says, "All things are lawful but not all things are helpful" (I Cor. 6:12, 10:23). Then to the same Corinthians he says, "To each is given the manifestation of the Spirit that is helpful" to him or her and to the Christian community (I Cor. 12:7). In contrast to the "spiritual life" of the Corinthians that was disrupting the community, Paul tells them of the gifts of the Spirit that are helpful to the building up of the church.

On the other hand, the fruit of the Spirit manifests itself in all the aspects of the life of believers. It shows itself in the "love, joy, peace, patience, kindness, goodness, faithfulness, gentleness, self-control" which characterize their lives (Gal. 5:22, 23). These things are not present in the lives of those who are under the power of "the flesh." They can only manifest themselves in those who have "crucified the flesh with its affections and lusts" and now belong to Christ (Gal. 5:24). Belonging to Christ and life in the Spirit, where the fruit of the Spirit may bloom, is the foundation of the Pauline ethic (Rom. 8:10). Paul does not move his thinking forward much beyond this point.[13]

LOVE AS THE EXPRESSION OF LIFE

If one wishes to have Paul say something more as to how the Christian life is to be lived, then one must note how he relates life in and by the Spirit with love. Several texts attest to this connection in the apostle's thought. As just noticed, when he enumerates the different manifestations of the fruit of the Spirit, Paul mentions love first. It would be difficult to argue that the list gives the characteristics of the fruit of the Spirit in order of importance. Yet it is significant that love is the first one mentioned. That "the love of the Spirit" (genitive of source) is something dear to the Christian is demonstrated by the fact that when Paul appeals to the Christians in Rome to join him in praying to God on his own behalf he bases his appeal on "our Lord Jesus Christ" and "the love of the Spirit" (Rom. 15:30). Christ and the love of the Spirit belong together; both are essential to the Christian life. Thus, among the many things that the Spirit has done and continues to do on behalf of Christians, Paul gives preeminence to the fact that the Spirit pours out God's love (Rom. 5:5).

As a motivational force for action, what could be more effective than God's love? It is this new factor in the life of Christians that makes for the difference between Christian conduct and any other kind of conduct. The possibility for Christian conduct is dependent upon the activity of the Spirit that pours out God's love in the hearts of those who, having been justified by faith, now have peace with God through the Lord Jesus Christ (Rom. 5:1).

Just as the Lord Jesus Christ and the love of the Spirit (or the love of God) go together in Paul's thought, so also do "the fellowship of the Spirit" and "the comfort of love" (Phil 2:1). Appealing to the Philippians to be of one mind and to let that one mind be the mind of Christ, Paul bases his entreaty on their experience of the fellowship of the Spirit and the comfort of love together with the consolation in Christ. These three things form the foundation of Christian unity in the concrete situations of Christian communities located in cities scattered all over the Roman world. Christian unity is not some monumental ideal to be expressed in dogmatic agreements and visions of ecclesiastical reorganizations. Whatever is to happen in the church has to be the work of God through his creative power. The working out of Christian unity in concrete communities of people is the work of "the love of the Spirit" or, as expressed in the letter to the Colossians, "the love *in* the Spirit" (Col. 1:8), that is, the love that those who live in the Spirit have for one another.

It is clear that Paul understands love to have its origin in God.[14] It is only God's love working itself out in the death of

Jesus that has achieved the salvation of men and women and concretizes itself even now in the love that Christians express toward one another. The Christian enjoys the perception that he is loved. Certainly, he loves God, but more importantly he knows himself loved by God. It is somewhat of a startling discovery to note that Paul, and to a large degree the whole of the New Testament, does not instruct Christians that their duty is to love God. Paul asks people to believe in, to obey, to fear, to know, to wait for, to trust in, to pray to God, but not primarily to love God. What people must realize is that God in Christ loved them. In fact, God in Christ "demonstrates his love for us in that while we were yet sinners Christ died for us" (Rom. 5:8). Paul had felt that love personally. He confesses that "the life I now live in the flesh I live by faith in the Son of God who loved me and gave himself for me" (Gal. 2:20). In a special sense, therefore, the members of the Christian communities are "the beloved of God" (I Thess. 1:4), and God is "the God of love and peace" (II Cor. 13:11).

The basic threat to the Christian life is that somehow, by some means, the Christian should cease to feel himself loved and thus be separated from the love of Christ (Rom. 8:35). Paul can think of a number of things that could attempt to produce just such a result. First, he lists adverse circumstances that may be concomitant with the life of discipleship in the flesh: "tribulation, distress, persecution, famine, nakedness, peril, or sword." All these vicissitudes may make the Christian life seem unrealistic in the world of sin. Concerning these, however, Paul exclaims "in all these things we are more than conquerors through him that loved us." In other words, these things are not strong enough to break the cords of love that hold the Christian bound to Christ. The Christian's enemies are conquered by the very love that they wish to defeat.

There are, however, many other enemies of a different kind which the Christian must face. These also wish to separate believers from the love of Christ. They are supernatural forces of the spirit world. They are "something else" within the creation in which men and women live. They operate in the heavenly realms of a fallen creation. Paul describes them as "angels," "principalities," "powers," "height," "depth." As to these Paul reinforces his confidence by declaring, "For I am sure that neither (of these) will be able to separate us from the love of God in Christ Jesus our Lord" (Rom.

8:39). In the realm of the spirit nothing is stronger than the love of God.

For Paul, the Christian who has been freed from the law is not free from every exterior force. Even if the law of the Spirit of life is primarily an interior power energizing the Christian life from within, the Christian is still bound by an exterior binding force, more binding than any written law. Christians are under the constraints of the love of Christ (II Cor. 5:14). This has an immediate and obvious corollary: under the constraints of the one who "loved me and gave himself for me" Christians cannot live for themselves. In view of the fact that Christ died for all, those who have believed in Christ's death and resurrection as God's act for the salvation of all mankind must now live out their own lives in testimony to the world of the effectiveness of God's righteousness. The love of Christ constrains the Christian to live for the neighbor on whose behalf Christ already died (II Cor. 5:15).

This means that the Christian is bound to extend God's salvation to his neighbor, and it is impossible for love to wrong a neighbor (Rom. 13:10). Paul reminded both the Corinthians and the Romans that Christian conduct controlled by love cannot injure the neighbor "for whom Christ died" (Rom. 14:15; I Cor. 8:11). The greatest expression of love is seen in conduct that is a translation of God's love toward the world for the benefit of the members of society with whom a Christian is in touch. Therefore, Christians who disregard the effect that their actions may have on their neighbors are no longer conducting themselves according to love (Rom. 14:15). If applied by Christians, the effects of this ethic would indeed bring about a different society.

The preposition "according to" (*kata*) is used by Paul in a most telling way. He clearly makes a distinction between life *in* the flesh, and life *according to* the flesh. The first is natural and unavoidable. Even Christ lived *in* the flesh, *under* the law, that is to say, he was born into the natural world as a Jew. But he did not live *according to* the flesh or *according to* the law. Either one of these two ways of life would have been considered by Paul as sinful. Christians must live *according to* love. That is to say, according to what is demanded to extend the love of God to their neighbors and bring about their salvation. The Christian ethic of love does not say that the action of Christians is determined by the situation in which they may find themselves. Rather, it says that the action of Christians is determined by God's ultimate will for their neighbors. The Christians who can no longer live for themselves act so as to establish in their neighbors an experience of the love of God. In this way Christians do not save their neighbors themselves Christ already died for all, including their neighbors. All that Christians can do is to demonstrate by their lives what in fact God has done already, since they are beneficiaries of the gift of the Spirit and life. It is because of this that "love is the fulfilling of the law" (Rom. 13:10), and that "he that loves his neighbor has fulfilled the law" (Rom. 13:8). Christians must continually conduct themselves with their neighbors "according to love" because love is what produces faith,[15] and how could a Christian bring about faith in a neighbor if he is not demonstrating God's love? Christians who do not "walk in love" (Rom. 14:15) prevent their neighbors from acting "from faith" (Rom. 14:23), and in this way they keep their neighbors in sin (Rom. 14:23). Such conduct is contrary to the Christian ethic that aims only at the neighbor's salvation.

FAITH HOPE AND LOVE

Paul's evaluation of the manifestation of God's love as the ultimate achievement possible to a human being contrasts quite sharply with many modern presentations of Paul as a preacher of righteousness by faith. As argued in a previous chapter, righteousness is a metaphor among others. When the apostle sets up faith, hope, and love in order to extol their importance in the life of Christians, he pronounces the judgment "but the greatest of these is love" (I Cor. 13:13).

Why is love greater than faith and hope? The short answer is because love is the source of both. Thus, when faith and hope cease to be exercised in a life of perfect fulfillment in an eschatological existence, love will continue to bind the Creator to his creatures. Love not only has to do with the way in which people live before God, but also with the way in which they relate to every other being. Faith and hope always carry with them an intellectualistic temptation, but love is indissolubly tied to the center of life itself.

The intellectualistic temptation of faith had overtaken the gnostics at Corinth. They trusted in their knowledge of God in order to defend a particular way of life both in church and in society. They lived under the slogan "We have knowledge" (I Cor. 8:1), and the corollary to that slogan was, therefore, "All things are lawful" (I Cor. 6:12; 10:23). To them Paul said, "If one loves God, one is known by him" (I Cor. 8:3). God is not captured by human knowledge or by human faith. A Christian's participation in the life of the Spirit, which is life in God, is only evident by the life of love that reveals God's knowledge of that individual. Knowledge and faith may be attempts to possess God, but a Christian's religious claims are tested by the way in which he/she lives out of love in the community. Therefore, Paul's ultimate command is "pursue love" (I Cor. 14:1).

The encapsulation of the Pauline ethic has not lacked detractors. It is not uncommon for those who preach a humanistic ethic to ridicule the ethic of love as the ethic of passivity, or the ethic of resignation. By contrast, an ethic for our time, we are told, must take the initiative; it must be an ethic of courage. True morality is to be judged by its purposefulness, and must not be a victim of circumstances. Twentieth century humanists who claim Nietzsche as their spiritual father work on the presupposition that the future of humanity is in human hands and cannot admit that the origin and goal of humanity is to be based on God's love.

At the center of Paul's exposition of the superiority of love are found the words "love bears all things, believes all things, hopes all things, endures all things" (I Cor. 13:7). At first glance these phrases would seem to substantiate the charge that love represents a passive attitude toward life. But these four phrases must be understood together in terms of well-known patterns of Semitic chiasmic parallelism. The first two terms speak of the present: love bears, love believes. The second terms move the thought forward toward the future in an inverted sequence: love hopes, love carries on.

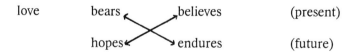

Together the four clauses interact to bring out the sense of stability and purposefulness embedded in love. Love is not shaky, love is not insecure, love is not passive, love does not settle down for the *status quo*, love is not a receptacle for things as they are. Paul cannot be charged with an ethic of passivity. His is not the Stoic ethic of emotional detachment (*ataraxia*). For him love is positive, love is inventive, love is full of surprises, love is full of miracles because it is grounded on God himself.

Love is not resignation to fate. Love is not what allows a man or a woman to accept life as it comes. Love hopes and carries on. Love is strength to accept the unbearable. Love is believing when the world provides no reasons. Love is hoping when the present does not warrant hope. Love is perseverance when the flesh is weak. Christian love is what gives a man or a woman a foundation on which to stand in all circumstances, but it is also a launching pad from which to reach out to the very source of life. Love does not bear, believe, hope and endure because it is stupid, gullible, unrealistic or submissive to the point of irresponsibility. Love bears, believes, hopes and endures because it is grounded on God and embraces all life.

To say that love believes and hopes is to say that, in him who hopes and believes, faith and hope arise from love. One may be unable to love everybody, but for those one does not have love, one does not have faith or hope either. To say that love bears and endures is to say that, in him who endures and bears, perseverance and strength arise from love. One may not carry everybody's burdens and keep alive everybody's struggles, but he who loves must take the realities of the world in a concrete way, "bearing" and "enduring."

In all its manifestations Christian love is one and the same because it is grounded in the unity of life in the Spirit. What is love if not the recognition that the vitality to live comes from a source which is not one's own? What is love if not the drive on the part of a creature to be reunited with the source of life? As an object of intellectual analysis, as the driving force of an ethical system, as a religious principle, as a human or a divine passion, love is the striving of the estranged to be reunited. As an emotion love anticipates the joy of reunion.

It has been said that what sets apart Christianity at the highest level among all religions, and at the same time distinguishes Western from Eastern cultures, is that Christianity while proclaiming love to be the highest manifestation of humanity's sharing in the life of God still preserves the individuality of all lovers. Love binds together but does not blend together. It brings about a fusion but not confusion. Lovers do not desire to absorb the other. That would be to lose the other. Lovers wish to preserve and to save the other. Love brings about unity but not uniformity. Love shapes and forms but not by imposing conformity to static forms.[16]

God's gift of love may be received with expressions of thanksgiving because the Gospel says that by giving mankind of Himself and by making in Christ a new creation, God was not absorbing mankind but reconciling mankind to Himself (II Cor. 5:17, 19). The new creation brought about by love, under whose control Christians live (II Cor. 5:14), is not an amorphous conglomerate of passive robots who do God's will *en masse*. The Christian life of the new creation is not the boring life of perfection on this earth but the exciting life of loving in the midst of enemies (Rom. 5:10). The Christian life is an extension of God's act of reconciliation.

One of the recurring spiritual temptations besetting Christians since Paul's day until our own has been to reduce the ethic of love to an ethic of perfection.[17] Such a view propagates the notion that Christians may escape the evil world in which they live by achieving a state of spiritual perfection. In other words, those who are truly filled with the Spirit manifest the life of the Spirit by perfect obedience to the law. But such a view interprets Christian freedom as freedom in the law when its demands are met, a view which is certainly not Pauline. Paul was not a preacher of freedom *in* the law but of freedom *from* the law. Paul did not preach perfection as defined by law. As far as he was concerned the only thing the law could define was sin. Paul reminded those who were tempted by visions of perfection as defined by law that according to that standard he would certainly qualify as perfect, but even if at one time in his life he might have succumbed to that temptation, ever since he had come to know Christ he had considered all that "perfection" as dung (Phil 3:4-11).

As Paul explains it to the Philippians, if the Christian strives to attain something it is not perfection in the law but the resurrection from the dead (Phil. 3:11). Christian perfection is not religious but eschatological. In the meantime, the apostle confides, he is neither living after a chimera, nor thinking that he has already attained it. Rather he lives knowing that Christ has made him his own, and, therefore, he strives toward a very different prize. His goal is not perfection in this life. His goal is to live in answer to a call from on high (Phil. 3:12-14). The ethic of answering the call of God is the ethic of love as the response to love. It is the ethic that pursues love. Paul is a realist. The Christian does not live sinlessly in the flesh. The Christian lives by love in the Spirit as to attain the resurrection from the dead.

CHAPTER VIII

THE LORD AND THE SLAVE

What to Paul may have been of first importance has been left here for the concluding chapter. The purpose for this has been the desire to leave the reader with a strong sense of what was at the center of Paul's thought. As pointed out, in the Book of Acts Paul is not designated as an apostle (the one exception is Acts 14:4, 14), since the title is reserved for the leaders of the Jerusalem community. As is well known, however, Paul always identified himself as an apostle, and as such he saw himself primarily as a *slave*. Slaves of divinities were not unknown to the Hellenistic world.[1] The story of the slave girl in Philippi who followed Paul and Barnabas for several days shouting, "These men are slaves of the Most High God, who proclaim to you the way of salvation" (Acts 16:17) makes the point well enough, even if Luke's theology of the "way of salvation" is also in evidence. According to the narrative, Paul became annoyed by her conduct and exorcised her demon. Still, in his own letters Paul insisted on identifying himself as "a slave of the Lord." That he did understand himself in this way is all the more remarkable when it is kept in mind that he lived in a society that practised slavery, and that he came from a family that belonged to the slave-owning class.

MY LORD

As a child of a Jewish upper middle-class family of the Diaspora, Paul must have come into close contact with family slaves. Depending on how old he was when he left home for Jerusalem, it may be inferred that after having reached a certain age he may have himself exercised the master's authority over a slave. Since childhood he must have enjoyed the benefits of having

138

household slaves performing their assigned tasks so that their masters might enjoy a more comfortable life. His own references to the relationship of minors, and young adults, to slaves may reflect Paul's own recollections (Gal. 3:25; 4:2). If his life had followed the course to which he seemed predestined by birth and upbringing, he would have been among the "masters" in Hellenistic society. His social prejudices, in spite of his Christian conversion, show him to have been a man of the upper class, well educated, quite literate, with certain condescending attitudes toward manual labor, and not concerned to address the reality of slavery as a social evil or a human injustice.[2]

Yet Paul was not to be a master. Having received the call to be an apostle for Christ, he found his Master and became the slave not only of Christ but of all men and women as well. God remained the same one and only God, but something more had come to be recognized by Paul about Him. He was "God and Father" (II Cor. 11:31; I Thess. 3:11), and "the One who raised Jesus from the dead" (I Cor. 6:14, II Cor. 4:14). God's Son is the Lord Jesus Christ (I Cor. 1:9), who is in the process of bringing all things into subjection to Himself (Phil. 3:21) in order to deliver all things to the overall dominion of God Himself (I Cor. 15:28). Having recognized the dominion of the Father and the Son, Paul immediately placed himself as an obedient servant at their command (II Cor. 10:5, Gal. 1:10). For him Jesus became "my Lord" (Phil. 3:8).

According to usage in the Jewish synagogue, "my Lord" designated Yahweh, whose name was too sacred to be pronounced. In order to avoid the inadvertent transgression of the third commandment, Jews still do not name God, either in their private and social conversations or in their worship services. Even in the reading of the Old Testament the word Yahweh is read as "Adonai," that is "my Lord." Already the Septuagint translators of the Old Testament had rendered Yahweh as "Kyrios," Lord. Thus when Paul uses Old Testament passages, either quoting or paraphrasing, he consistently designates Yahweh as "*Kyrios*," Lord (Rom. 4:8; 9:28f.; 10:13; 11:5, 34; 12:19; 14:11; 15:11; I Cor. 1:31; 2:16, 10:26; 14:21; II Cor. 6:17; 10:17). But it is clear that on his own, when not referring to scriptural passages, Paul also uses the expression Lord to designate God Himself (I. Cor. 10:9; 22: I Thess. 4:6). In a few instances, however, it is not quite clear whether by Lord he is referring to God or Jesus Christ (i.e., II Cor. 3:16; 5:11).

Most often, however, even when not specifying "the Lord Jesus" or "the Lord Jesus Christ," when Paul says "the Lord" it is clear that he means the crucified and risen One. As such, the early Christian confession "Jesus is Lord" was already well established among Christians before Paul's call. It already occupied a prominent place in the pre-Pauline hymn to Christ found in Philippians 2. Paul's letters, moreover, make clear that he found this way of looking at Jesus particularly significant and that a person's attachment to Him as the Lord was basic to the Christian life (I Cor. 12:32; II Cor. 4:5). To believe Him to be such with the mind, or the heart, and to confess Him with the lips (or the body?) is the clear sign that the Gospel has effectively exercised its power to save (Rom. 10:9).

LORD IN THE RELIGIOUS VOCABULARY

The very influential study on the title "Lord Christ" done by Wilhelm Bousset at the turn of the century,[3] made it standard practice to understand the title Lord as one which Gentile Christians popularized. They avoided the more Jewish and apocalyptic title that had been used by the first Christian believers in Palestine: Son of Man. Lord, it was argued, had its origins in the practice of the mystery religions popular in the Roman Empire in the first century. Newly converted Christians were used to speaking of their former pagan gods as Lord Serapis, or Lord Osiris. They were the ones who introduced the title Lord Christ into the Christian vocabulary. In this way, they also shifted Christianity away from its apocalpytic concentration on the return of the Son of Man and focused attention on mystical union with the Lord during this life. It may very well have been the case that Christians of pagan background found it congenial to their religious manner of speaking to refer to the Jewish Messiah as Lord Jesus. It is, however, also true that Paul's usage of the title Lord is not a way of rejecting the apocalyptic vision of the Sovereign of the Universe in order to concentrate on a mystical union with Him in this life. The Pauline vision of the Lord is closely related to the vision of the world as existing under the powers of good and evil who are at the moment struggling for control over the affairs of the world. Paul expects the final resolution of this struggle to take place momentarily.

To proclaim Jesus as Lord was to proclaim that the struggle between good and evil had been decided. The god of this aeon (II Cor. 4:40), Satan (II Cor. 2:11; 11:14), had been defeated at Jesus' cross and resurrection. The love (Rom. 5:8) and the power (I Cor. 6:4) of God had been demonstrated in the creation of a new aeon in which "Jesus Christ is our Lord" (I Cor. 1:8; 5:5; II Cor. 8:9; I Thess. 2:19; Phil. 3:20).[4]

As Lord, Jesus Christ has established a new creation within which the Christian community lives under its Lord. In the meantime the unbelievers, who do not accept Jesus Christ as Lord, live under other lords (I Cor. 8:5) and demons (I Cor. 10:21). These alternatives are repeatedly presented by Paul as mutually exclusive. Men and women must choose to which Lord they will be enslaved. As creatures they live within a creation. They are either slaves of sin or slaves of righteousness (Rom. 6:16, 17). Individuals may hide the identity of their lord with some degree of success. Servants of Satan may be successful in disguising themselves as servants of rightousness (II Cor. 11:15). But in this they are only following the example of their lord, who is guile personified. He pretends to be an angel of light, but the disguise of the master disguiser and his servants will be exposed when at the end they will be judged according to their deeds.

On the other hand, the slaves of the Lord Jesus Christ follow the example of their Lord, who even though he was God became a slave obedient unto death. For Paul this is the model for his ministry. His Lord is the conqueror of sin and death. Consequently, as His ambassador he is not a junior lord but a slave. Christ's own lordship, by the power of his resurrection, was the result of his having served as a slave at the cross. Paul chose to become a slave and be crucified with Christ daily in order to live with Christ (Gal. 2:20). Through Christ he had now become a slave of all men and women (II Cor. 4:5).

THE PARADOX OF MINISTRY

The polarity between the lord and the slave is intimately related to the apparent incongruity of power in weakness. The apostle conceives his sufferings, his many beatings, shipwrecks, the dangers of his journeys by land and sea, his having had to flee many cities under cover, his having had to toil while hungry and thirsty, as evidences of his weakness. These were the things that identified him as a faithful servant of Christ (II Cor. 11:23, 30). Had he been strong, or powerful, he would not have had to undergo any of these many hardships and humiliations. He would have been able to move around as a powerful official. His weakness was the evidence of his slavery to the accomplishment of a task for Christ. To talk about it is not to talk "according to the Lord" (II Cor. 11:17), but to speak as other apostles who boast "according to the flesh" (II Cor. 11:18). Paul considered it sheer folly "to boast of the things that show my weakness." His characterization of his weakness, however, provides us with one of the most revealing passages concerning his own self-understanding. By weakness he means the manner of his ministry, the humble and precarious nature of his work, and his own inability as a slave of Christ to work "in the grand manner."

Christ is the Lord, and lordship is supported by power. Throughout his letters Paul spoke of the power of God, of Christ, of the Holy Spirit, and of the resurrection (i.e., II Cor. 13:4; 12:9; I Cor. 1:24; 2:25; Phil. 3:10). He also wrote of the Gospel, the cross, and the Kingdom of God as the power of God (Rom. 1:16; I Cor. 1:18; 4:20). As conceived by Paul, God's power was demonstrated in creation and in redemption. He "gives life to the dead and calls into existence the things that do not exist" (Rom. 4:17). In the cross, in the resurrection, and in the Gospel, this power is at work "for salvation." Now the spreading of the Gospel among the nations is an extension of God's saving activity by the power required for its effectiveness. This is why the Spirit, who is Himself the power of God, is indispensable in the annunciation of the Gospel. The effectiveness of the preaching is not dependent upon the power of the preacher but upon the activity of the Spirit. The "authority" of the preacher is not certified by his display of power but by whether or not his hearers receive the Spirit. It is clear, then, that Paul intended power to mean what God is or does that brings about salvation to persons. This power had been experienced by Paul in his own life and in that of the community, but only in relationship to weakness. The Lord does not work through junior lords but through slaves.

According to Paul, his triple plea to be relieved from "his thorn in the flesh" received an oracular answer from the Lord,

"My grace is sufficient for you, for my power is made perfect in weakness" (II Cor. 12:9). Does this mean that unless weakness is present the power of God may not be perceived, in which case weakness serves to reveal the activity of the power of God? Or does it mean that unless there is weakness there may not be power, in which case weakness and power are related to each other in the order of reality rather than in the order of knowledge? Is Paul setting forth a general principle that is true in the lives of all Christians who serve Christ while waiting for the Parousia? Or is Paul speaking autobiographically?[5]

From the context, it is clear that Paul saw his own weakness as a participation in the weakness of Christ (II Cor. 13:4). That was how he was "always being given up to death for Jesus' sake" (II Cor. 4:11). The notion that trials, misfortunes, sickness, etc. are already forms of death or at least a diminishment of life is well known in the Old Testament. Sickness, poverty, or social and political powerlessness represent either the arms of Sheol reaching out to embrace and swallow its victims or to be brought by God to the very gates of Sheol. On the other hand, health, wealth, and general prosperity reflect a strong connection with the living God.[6]

Paul understood his weakness, however, not in connection with the power of Sheol but in connection with the cross of Christ (II Cor. 13:4). For him weakness was essential to his Christology. He was weak because he participated, while serving his Lord, in his Lord's cross (Gal. 4:14). His service was patterned after that of Christ. His apostleship, like Christ's sojourn on earth, was characterized by his not having claimed the perquisites that normally would have been considered his (I Cor. 9:1-18). If he said, "Be imitators of me," it was only in reference to this attitude, which he learned from his Lord. That is why he adds "as I am of Christ" (Cor. 11:1). It is this posture in life, which is so powerfully described in the Christ hymn of Philippians 2:6-11, that he wishes all Christians to adopt as their (Phil. 2:5 and *passim*). The perfection of power in weakness may be understood only in terms of the perfection of the cross at Easter (II Cor: 13:4). It cannot, therefore, be said that this is an autobiographical insight on Paul's part. It is rather an insight into the way in which the new aeon came into being. It is built into the structure of the new aeon. God's power manifests itself only in those who recognize themselves as his slaves and, therefore, claim nothing for themselves. It is only in full confidence of what the Lord has accomplished, rather than in their ability to carry it out, that His servants undergo the trials of life. They are no longer rooted in the ways in which their cultures operate or are supported by their structures. The power of God is what continues to uphold their lives and gives them whatever success they attain.

Paul's ministry as an apostle is planned and executed to capitalize on the new structure of things. To the Corinthian "spirituals," who thought themselves wise, he said, "I was with you in weakness and in much fear and trembling, and my speech and my message were not in plausible words of wisdom, but in demonstrations of the Spirit and power that your faith might not rest in the wisdom of men, but in the power of God" (I Cor. 2:4f.). Paul is perfectly aware that the extraordinary power that brings about the expansion of the kingdom by the creation of believers is the power of God, working through the Spirit. The balance necessary for the operation of this power through the weakness of the slave of Christ is in itself the achievement of the Spirit. That the difficulties, trials, fear and trembling of the apostle do not culminate in despair and defeat is nothing short of a miracle fully attributable to the working of the Spirit. That the slave is preserved, rather than destroyed, by the very service that he renders "in the Lord" is in itself a demonstration of the authenticity of his service.[7]

Psychological explanations of the Christian's weakness, or moral lessons derived from it, are only a caricature of what Paul is concerned with. The manifestation of power in weakness is not so that men and women may learn a moral lesson or come to realize their impotence before the burden of their sins. Rather, the context is that of the powerful agents of God who extend the benefits of salvation to mankind, not in a triumphalist manner but as slaves. The cross they carry is the cross of their Lord, but they carry it in their own society and their own culture as their own cross. If the cross reveals him/her as weak, it must not be forgotten that it also reveals the power of God. It was the Lord who was crucified on it (I Cor. 2:8). Salvation is in the Lord's death (I Cor. 11:26), not in the power of the messengers.[8]

Paul is careful to keep things in their proper relationship. He insists, "What we preach is not ourselves, but Jesus Christ as Lord, with ourselves as your servants for Jesus' sake" (II Cor.

4:5). If his life was in weakness and power, it was because he was living out the weakness and power of Christ's death and resurrection. Such, by the very nature of the aeon of the Lord, must be what characterizes the lives of all those who live in the body of Christ.

In Paul's mind the power of the new aeon is associated with the Spirit. By contrast with the fallen creation which is flesh and therefore weak, the Spirit who inaugurated the new aeon is power. Explicitly, Paul never equates God's Spirit with His power. Still, the two are conceived as closely tied together. Their connection is especially to be seen in the eschatological event of the cross and the resurrection, which, as in the creation of the heavens and the earth, were brought about by the Spirit. It is the presence of the Spirit that guarantees new life in the new aeon (Rom. 8:11).

MINISTRY AND ITS TRIALS

The authenticity of Paul's apostleship, as far as we know, was challenged primarily at Thessalonica, Corinth, and Galatia.[9] To defend his apostleship to the Corinthians, who made many disqualifying charges against him, Paul ultimately resorts "to boast in his weakness," even if to do that is not quite "according to the Lord." The list of charges against Paul at Corinth included the following items: When present he is weak and humble, when away he becomes bold and sends threatening letters (II Cor. 10:1, 10). He is not subject to Christ because he likes to impose himself on others, thus overstepping his authority (II Cor. 10:7, 8). Compared to the "great" apostles, however, he is a nobody (II Cor. 10:12; 12:11). Actually, in trying to supervise the spiritual life of the Corinthians, he is overreaching himself since his territories do not include Europe (II Cor. 10:14). He really does not love the Corinthians because he does not accept financial support from them, even though he has accepted it from other churches (II Cor. 11:9, 11, 16). When he goes out and employs himself as an artisan, he makes a fool of himself and embarrasses the Corinthians (II Cor. 11:7.8). The only reason he was successful in converting them to his type of Christianity was that he used underhanded ways; he got the better of them by guile (II Cor. 12:16).

There is a bit of irony, if not sarcasm, in Paul's words. Had he actually done any or all of these things, he would have been conducting his ministry "according to the flesh." In other words, he would not be living in Christ at all. To be suspected of acting "according to the flesh" is the one thing he cannot tolerate. "For even if," he says, "we live in the flesh we are not fighting our battles according to the flesh. The weapons of our warfare are not fleshly but empowered by God" (II Cor. 10:3, 4, author's translation). To the Corinthians, who would disqualify him on account of his overbearing and overreaching illusions of grandeur, Paul by a solemn appeal ("the God and Father of the Lord Jesus, He who is blessed for ever, knows that I do not lie," II Cor. 11:31) boasts in the things that emphasize his weakness (II Cor. 11:30). The proof of his apostleship is none other than the conversion of the Corinthians themselves. To defend his apostleship he does not ultimately direct their attention to himself but to themselves: "You are the seal of my apostleship in the Lord" (I Cor. 9:1).

The Galatians disqualified Paul as an apostle for lack of proper credentials. He was not one of the original twelve. Apparently, he had been taught by some people somewhere. Therefore, he was teaching only to please those who had taught him the Gospel in the first place. To the Galatians Paul insists on the divine origin of his call and of his Gospel. He is not an apostle "from men nor through man, but through Jesus Christ and God the Father who raised him from the dead" (Gal. 1:1). What he preached was not what someone taught him but what came to him through a revelation of Jesus Christ (Gal. 1:11f.). It was true that he did not receive the Gospel from the Christian leaders in Jerusalem. He had not spent enough time with any of them to have received the Gospel from them. In seventeen years, after his call to the apostleship, he had spent only fifteen days in Jerusalem with Peter and James (Gal. 1:18; 2:1). When after seventeen years he went to Jerusalem for a second time, he did not go to learn the Gospel. He went to agree on a mission strategy with Peter, James, and John. That meeting ended with an exchange of the right hand of fellowship among all concerned, including Paul's companion Barnabas (Gal. 2:9). To the charges of the Galatians concerning his apostleship and the origin of his gospel, Paul answered with a contrary-to-fact conditional sentence and a rhetorical question. "If I were still pleasing men, I should not be a *slave* of Christ" (Gal. 1:10), and "If I . . . still preach circumcision, why am I still persecuted?" (Gal.

5:11). As a matter of fact, he is a slave of Christ; therefore, he is still being persecuted because he has not been working to please men, and, therefore, he has not given in to the pressure of Jewish Christians who preach salvation through the law.

BEING IN THE LORD

It is not only in his activity as an apostle engaged in the proclamation of the Gospel that the slave-Lord relationship is manifested. Whatever Christians are or do they are or do "in the Lord Jesus Christ." Paul's apostleship is "in the Lord" (I Cor. 9:2). Timothy is faithful "in the Lord." The man-and-wife marriage relationship is "in the Lord" (I Cor. 11:11). Those who are in charge of the churches are leaders "in the Lord" (I Thess. 5:12; II Cor. 10:8; 13:10). Tryphaena and Tryphosa are "workers in the Lord" and the beloved Persis has "worked hard in the Lord" (Rom. 16:12), while Rufus is "eminent in the Lord" (Rom. 16:13). But in the family of Narcissus some are "in the Lord" while others are not (Rom. 16:11).

Paul's authority is "in the Lord" (II Cor. 10:8; 13:10). His comings and goings are "in the Lord" (II Cor. 2:12). Whatever confidence he has in the members of his congregations is "in the Lord" (Gal. 5:10; II Thess. 3:4). Whatever he is sure of "he knows and is persuaded in the Lord" (Rom. 14:14). Whatever he instructs, exhorts, or commands, he does "in the Lord" (I Thess. 4:1; II Thess. 3:6, 12).

The saints ought to do things "in the Lord" (Rom. 16:2). They are "elect in the Lord" (Rom. 16:13). They have been "called in the Lord" (I Cor. 7:22). Their "faith . . . love . . . and hope is in the Lord" (I Thess. 1:3). They must "stand firm in the Lord" (Phil. 4:1; I Thess. 3:8). They must have the same mind "in the Lord" (Phil. 4:2). Above all they must always "rejoice in the Lord" (Phil. 3:1; 4:4). In a word, Christians "live in the Lord" (Rom. 14:4). Thus the Pauline understanding of the relationship between the source and the means for Christian existence is well captured in the epigram "As therefore you received Christ Jesus the Lord, so live in him" (Col. 2:6).

As the Lord, Jesus Christ is to rule over those who live in him and who thereby are no longer ruled by sin (Rom. 5:21; 6:12).

If prior to their faith in Christ men and women were slaves of sin (Rom. 6:17, 20), captives of the law of sin and death (Rom. 7:6, 23; 8:2; Gal. 3:23), in bondage to "weak and beggarly elemental spirits" (Gal. 4:8f.), that is no longer the case for those who live "in the Lord." Jesus Christ means deliverance from the dominion of death. Christians no longer serve under the old written code, but rather they serve in the new life of the Spirit (Rom. 7:6).

Ultimately, the contrast is between slavery to death and slavery in life. Under the Lord Jesus Christ, Christians lead the lives assigned to them (I Cor. 7:17). Thus, even if there is One Lord, service under Him is not demonstrated by its monotonousness, its uniformity, its lack of individualizing characteristics. Rather, it is distinguished by its diversity in the One Lord (I Cor. 12:5). If there is one thing that makes the varieties of ministries equal under the Lord, it is their undivided devotion to the Lord (I Cor. 7:35). Unlike service to death, which is characterized by the corrosive presence of sin, service to Christ is characterized by its righteousness, peace and joy in the Holy Spirit and as such is acceptable to God and is approved by everyone (Rom. 14:17f.).

FREEDOM IN THE LORD

It is the Spirit that gives the service of the Lord its essential differentiation from service to death. Christians serve in the new life of the Spirit (Rom. 7:6). As already said above, the Spirit brings in the element of power in the weakness of the Christian life, but the Spirit also brings in the joy of the Christian life, and this joy is intimately associated with the particular quality of Christian existence in the Lord: slavery to Christ means freedom.

The anwser to the peculiar dialectic between the Lord and the slave in Paul's thought is found in his notion of freedom. In the presence of the Lord, being a slave does not mean slavery. In the Lord there can only be freedom. Slavery to the Lord of creation and redemption is freedom and ultimate glory. If Christians enjoy the only life in freedom possible on earth, it is so only to the degree in which they submit to the Lord of Life. Whether this interpretation of slavery is a way to avoid having to face the great social injustices current in his world or is due to his own social background, it is not possible to determine. Yet freedom as an eschatological reality represented for Paul the essential characteristic of a Christian life in this aeon. Since for him freedom is clearly a spiritual and eschatological condition, it is difficult to translate Paul's message into economic or political programs for human liberation based on the power of armies or the leverage of economic resources or international public opinion.

For Paul, freedom must be tied down to some specifics. Grammatically speaking, freedom must be followed by a preposition. One may be free from . . . in order to be free to . . . or free for. . . . Freedom is not something that stands on its own two feet. Freedom is not somewhere waiting for people to come and take shelter under it. Freedom is a possibility when it is protected or guaranteed. Therefore, freedom may only exist in communities. Within different communities, people may have the possibility for different kinds of freedoms. In other words, freedom is always relative in reference to its source or the power that establishes it. If freedom is to extend beyond the limits of a person's personal life, it must have its source outside that person. A freedom that originates within an individual is limited to that individual. A freedom that originates from a particular ideology like democracy, capitalism, or communism is relative to the limitations of its ideology. A freedom that has its sources in brute force, or military power, is limited to the might of that power. A freedom that is to bring about freedom from sin and freedom from death must have its source beyond the world of sin and death. For Paul, freedom in Christ is true freedom precisely because its source transcends all the limitations of the fallen creation. Freedom in Christ is freedom in the Creator Himself, under whom all things exist. It is in this context that Paul insists that Christians are not "born of a slave woman" (Gal. 4:3l). The source of freedom cannot be a slave mother. Christian freedom is not guaranteed by the law, but by Christ.

Life in the Lord is life in freedom because its source is the promise of God himself (Gal. 4:23). As a promise whose source is God and whose guarantee is the Spirit (II Cor. 5:5), the life of a Christian is constituted in a different reality and is characterized by a different quality: freedom.

To the Galatians the apostle insists that except for service to the Lord Christians cannot be in bondage to any thing in the realm of "this present evil aeon." The Lord Jesus Christ gave himself for their sins precisely in order to deliver men and women from the very power of sin (Gal. 1:3). As Paul insists, Christian freedom is "for freedom" (Gal. 5:1). In other words, to see the work of Christ within the general structures of the present aeon is to negate it. What Christ accomplished transcends the neat ways in which life may be conceived or regulated by religious means. Christian life cannot be contained, or preserved, by religious standards. It is "for freedom" in as much as it is "walked" by the Spirit (Gal. 5:25). That is the "truth of the Gospel" (Gal. 2:5, 14).

It should not be surprising, therefore, that Paul identifies the Lord and the Spirit in order to point out that the weakness, the suffering, the trials, the anxiety, the death that are always present in the service of Christ (I Cor. 4:9; II Cor. 4:8-12) are precisely the very manifestations not only of the power of God, but also of His freedom. "Now the Lord is the Spirit, and where the Spirit of the Lord is, there is freedom" (II Cor. 3:17). Clearly the freedom provided wherever the Spirit of the Lord is present is not the possession of any one Christian nor for that matter of the Christian community which is the temple of the Holy Spirit (I Cor. 3:16f.; 6:19f.). Only those who are "in the Lord" may know about Christian freedom. Freedom is present not where the Christian is present but where the Lord who is the Spirit is present. Christian freedom is always derived from the Lord who makes free those who walk in Him.[10]

It is under such a condition that the glory of the Lord is transferred by the Spirit from the Lord to the slave. The Christian hope is "to share in the glory of God" (Rom. 5:2), and the Gospel is being preached so that people may "obtain the glory of our Lord Jesus Christ" (II Thess. 2:14). But by the working of the Spirit, as they with unveiled faces (that is to say, in freedom) behold the glory of the Lord, Christians "are being changed into his likeness from one degree of glory to another" (II Cor. 3:18). This metamorphosis is the work of the Lord who is the Spirit. But the likeness of the Lord into which Christians are being changed is the likeness of His service at the cross. The different degrees of glory to which Christians attain as they are being changed from glory to glory are not stations on the road to heavenly glorification but stations on the road of self-giving to others in service for the Gospel of the cross (II Cor. 4:5).

Having been made free in Christ Jesus has removed all veils

that prevented an unobstructed view of God. It is this new vision of God as the Father of our Lord Jesus Christ that informs the life of Christians and delivers them from the deceptions of the rulers of this aeon (I Cor. 3:6, 8; II Cor. 4:4; 11:14f.). Their hearts have received the outpouring of God's love by the Spirit (Rom. 5:5). Renewed in this way, God himself can now shine in their hearts and give them "the light of the knowledge of the glory of God in the face of Christ" without mediators of any kind (II Cor. 4:6). This is the freedom of Christians: the freedom to an unmediated knowledge of the glory of God. But where is this knowledge found? Not in the face of Moses (II Cor. 3:7) but in the face of Christ (II Cor. 4:6). And what is it that the face of Christ, as distinct from the face of Moses, reveals? It reveals a crown of thorns (I Cor. 2:2). That is why Paul advises any one who wishes to have an opinion of him and of his co-workers to understand them "as slaves of Christ" (I Cor. 4:1). If they commend themselves in any way to anybody it is only "as slaves of God" (II Cor. 6:4). Moses may have been a great leader who triumphed over Pharaoh and commanded respect and attention. As the lawgiver and legislator he stands as the paragon of the man of God in Israel's consciousness. But Paul's ministry is not to be compared with Moses'. Paul had learned a lesson that is difficult to learn. It is only as slaves that "Christ leads us in triumph" (II Cor. 2:14).

As an ambassador for Christ (II Cor. 5:20) Paul sees his task as that of declaring what God had done in Christ. But as such he is not primarily revealing God's work. He is not the one through whom God's glory is revealed, as Moses was said to have been. He does communicate knowledge of the glory of God, but he does this only to the degree that by the Spirit of the living God he conducts himself as a faithful slave who is constrained by the love of his Lord (II Cor. 5:14). God's glory, however, does not shine now in him; it shines in the face of Christ (II Cor. 4:6). Conducting his service under the constraints of love, he has found freedom wherever the Spirit of the Lord is present (II Cor. 3:17). This freedom in his Lord is neither a psychological nor a social way of escaping responsibility. It is rather a vision of God that transcends the limitations of creatures of flesh since it is based on God's action in Christ. There is where the eschatological kingdom is established (II Cor. 5:18).

NOTES

Chapter I

1. Josephus, *Antiquities*, XIV. 200-212.

2. Jews were also exempt from homage to the emperor and from certain taxes. After A.D. 70, when Jews were no longer paying their tithes to the temple, Vespatian introduced the *fiscus judaicus*, which Jews sent to Rome rather than to Jerusalem.

3. This point is cogently argued by V. Tcherikover, Hellenistic *Civilization and the Jews*. H. Wolfson's presentation of Philo as an Alexandrian Jew who kept himself undefiled by contacts with Hellenistic cultural institutions (*Philo*, 1948) has been shown to be inadequate by A. Mendelson, "A Re-Appraisal of Wolfson's Method."

4. Strabo, *Geography*, XIV. v. 12-15.

5. W. C. van Unnik's argument for Paul's early upbringing in Jerusalem, even though provocative, remains unproven, *Tarsus or Jerusalem: The City of Paul's Youth*, 1962.

6. See N. Hugedé, *St Paul et la culture grècque*, 1966, and H. D. Betz. *Der Apostel Paulus und die sokratische Tradition*, 1972.

7. This has been argued convincingly by R. Hock, "Paul's Tent Making and the Problem of his Social Class," and more recently in *The Social Context of Paul's Ministry: Tent Making and Apostleship*, 1980.

8. Two versions of the legend about the origins of the Septuagint have survived. One is found in *The Letter of Aristeas*, and the other in Josephus, *Antiquities*, XII. 2. 1.

9. For a description of the Septuagint as a translation, see C. H. Dodd, *The Bible and the Greeks*, 1935.

10. In popular moral teaching the metaphor was used in reference to the conscience, Philo, *Det. Pot. Ins*, 146.

11. For a comparison of the lists of vices and virtues found in the New Testament epistles and those used in Hellenistic households see E. Schweizer, "Traditional Ethical Patterns in the Pauline and Post-Pauline Letters and their Development."

12. For a description of tolerance within Judaism see R. Jewett, *Christian Tolerance*, 1982.

13. Good examples are found in Rom. 4:3-25; I Cor. 10:1-14; II Cor. 3:7-18.

14. This view as first proposed by F. C. Baur, *Paul: The Apostle of Jesus Christ*, 1886. For recent proponents of this view see G. Bornkamm, *Paul*, 1971, 13-16, and J. C. Beker, *Paul the Apostle*, 1980, 143-44.

15. J. Weiss, *Earliest Christianity*, 1959, I, 187, and F.F. Bruce, *Paul: Apostle of the Heart Set Free*, 1977, 71.

16. For a rather imaginative assessment of Paul's psychological make-up see R. Rubinstein, *My Brother Paul*, 1972.

17. See M. Hengel, *The Charismatic Leader and His Followers*, 1981, 18-20.

18. Cf. M. Smith, "What is Implied by the Variety of Messianic Figures," 66, and G. Vermes, *Jesus the Jew: A Historian's Reading of the Gospel*, 1973, 35-36. R. Spivey and D. M. Smith affirm, "No record exists of any Jewish court ever condemning

anyone as a messianic pretender." *Anatomy of the New Testament*, 1974, 231.

19. Both F. Hahn, *The Titles of Jesus in Christology*, 1969, 168-72, and R. H. Fuller, *The Foundations of New Testament Christology*, 1965, 158-59, have argued that in the earliest period of the church the title *Messiah was not applied to Jesus.*

20. See M. *Wilcox*, "'Upon the Tree'--Deut. 21:22-23 in the New Testament," 85-99.

21. This point has been well argued by E. Sanders, *Paul and Palestinian Judaism*, 1978, *passim*.

22. See M. *Hengel, Crucifixion*, 1974, 1-10.

23. See A. Hultgren, "Paul's Pre-Christian Persecutions of the Church: Their Purpose, Locale and Nature," 98. There have been some efforts to deny that Jews ever persecuted Christians at this early time in the history of Christian-Jewish relations, but as M. Smith declares the persecution of Christians by Jews at that time "is too well attested to be denied." "The Reason for the Persecution of Paul and the Obscurity of Acts," 261.3

Chapter II

1. See E. Haenchen, *The Acts of the Apostles: A Commentary*, 1971, 90-110.

2. The contrast is distinctly drawn by K. Stendahl, *Paul Among the Jews and Gentiles*, 1976, 7-23.

3. For an analysis of the prophetic-call narratives in the Old Testament see, G. von Rad, *Old Testament Theology*, 1965, II, 50-69, and N. Habel, "The Form and Significance of the Call Narrative."

4. For explications of Paul's conversion as catharsis from the burdens of guilt, see B. W. Bacon, *The Story of St. Paul*, 1904, 38-39, and R. Rubinstein, *My Brother Paul*, 41. N. Perrin's words are typical, "Haunted by the sense of stain, of guilt, of defilement, Paul searches for the means of cleansing, of expiation, of redemption, and he finds it in Christ and his Cross," *The New Testament: An Introduction*, 1974, 306.

5. From among the early disciples and apostles, only of Paul is there a definite reference to his baptism (Acts 9:18, 22:16). Later generations of Christians have been intrigued by the silence in the record about the baptism of the twelve. See E. H. Kantorowicz, "The Baptism of the Apostles."

6. For a view of the religion of Paul as a mysticism oriented toward Christ, see W. Bousset, *Kyrios Christos*, 1970, A. Schweitzer, *The Mysticism of Paul*, 1931, and A. Deissmann, *Paul: A Study in Social and Religious History*, 1912.

7. See P. S. Minear, "Dear Theo: The Kerygmatic Intention and Claim of the Book of Acts," C. H. Talbert, "Promise and Fulfilment in Lucan Theology," and J. T. Sanders, "The Salvation of the Jews in Luke Acts."

8. G. Bornkamm, *Paul*, 25.

9. Ch. I, pp. 10-13.

10. Ch. II, p. 2.

11. For the initial redactional evaluation of the evidence, see H. Conzelmann, *The Theology of St. Luke*, 1961, 73ff.

12. For an excellent discussion of the prophetic tensions with the centers of religious authority, see J. Blenkinsopp, *Prophecy and Canon*, 1977, 142-47.

13. I find it impossible to verify from the evidence F. F. Bruce's statement, "Paul appears to have esteemed the Jerusalem

Church and its leaders more highly than they esteemed him," *Men and Movements in the Primitive Church*, 1979, 101.

14. See C. K. Barrett, "Paul and the 'Pilar Apostles'."

15. As suggested by C. K. Barrett, the animosity manifested in Paul's struggles with "the false apostles" may be due to the fact that Paul sees them within the complex of "an eschatological phenomenon," *Essays on Paul*, 1982, 103.

16. See C. K. Barrett, "The Allegory of Abraham, Sarah and Hagar in the Argument of Galatians," *Essays on Paul*, 154-70.

17. A.D. Nock, *St. Paul*, 1963, 80.

18. For a review of alternative solutions and a bibliography see P. Feine, J. Behm, W. G. Kümmel, *Introduction to the New Testament*, 1966, 128-32.

19. For an argument against seeing the division of labor set along geographical lines, see P. Bowers, "Paul and Religious Propaganda in the First Century."

20. I Thess. 2:14-16 contains an enigmatic reference to some persecution suffered by Paul from his Jewish brethren in Judea. When this took place and who were the ones trying to prevent Paul from preaching to Gentiles is not clear. The evidence seems to indicate that Paul did not receive much support for his mission to the Gentiles from Jerusalem. Paul's understanding of how God was extending salvation to all humankind on a new basis seems to have been strongly opposed by some Jewish Christians. All this explains why Jerusalem never was Paul's Christian home.

21. Since the Book of Acts knows nothing about the collection, it cannot be said that "*the Jerusalem Church refused to accept the collection*," J. D. G. Dunn, *Unity and Diversity in the New Testament*, 1977, 257 (italics his). For the significance of the role played by the collection see K. F. Nickle, *The Collection: A Study in Paul's Strategy*, 1966.

22. See E. Pagels, *The Gnostic Paul: Gnostic Exegesis of the Pauline Letters*, Philadelphia: Fortress, 1975.

23. Mk. 2:21,22//Mt. 9:16,17//Lk. 5:36,37.

24. Several recent studies have argued that Christian missionaries are to be understood as engaging in public religious propaganda after the manner which characterized the cynic philosophers of the time. See, however, S. K. Stowers, "Social Status, Public Speaking and Private Teaching: The Circumstances of Paul's Preaching Activity," who argues that Paul was not a street-corner preacher sophist. As an artisan he would have lacked the necessary status required to speak at public places. His preaching, therefore, must have been centered in private homes.

25. See O. F. A. Mainhardus, "Paul's Missionary Journey to Spain: Tradition and Folklore," 61-63.

26. There are two excellent studies of Paul's chronology available. Their authors, however, are over-optimistic about their ability to pinpoint events in time: R. Jewett. R. Jewett, *A Chronology of Paul's Life*, 1979, and G. Ludemann, *Paul, Apostle to the Gentiles: Studies in Chronology*, 1984.

27. We seem to have three letters of Paul to the Corinthians in which he instructs them about the how and the why of the collection: 1 Cor 16, II Cor. 8, and II Cor. 9.

28. Defending himself from Tertullus' accusations before the procurator at Caesarea, Luke has Paul say, "I came to bring to my nation alms and offerings. As I was doing this, they found me purified in the temple" (Acts 24: 17f.). If this is a reference to the collection at all, it represents a clear misunderstanding of its purpose, or Luke's vague knowledge of it is being put to serve his own purposes.

29. E.g., G. Bornkamm, *Paul*, 100.

30. Two such warning signs have been recovered by archae-
ologists. See J. Finegan, *The Archaeology of the New Testament*,
1969, 119-20.

31. For a review of the arguments for other prisons as
possible places of origin for these epistles, see Feine-Behm- Kümmel,
Introduction to the New Testament, 229-35.

32. A most interesting analysis of the battle for control
over the Pauline tradition is to be found in D. R. MacDonald, *The
Legend and the Apostle: The Battle for Paul in Story and Canon*,
1983.

33. Caius, *Againt Proclus*, quoted by Eusebius, *Ecclesiastical
History*, II, xxv. 7.3

Chapter III

1. See W.S. Campbell, "Some Recent Literature on Paul's
Letter to the Romans: A Critical Survey,"   J. C. Beker, *Paul the
Apostle*, 59-93, and R. Jewett, "Major Impulses in the Theological
Interpretation of Romans since Barth."

2. This is particularly apparent in 2:17-3:20; 4:1-25; 7:1-25;
9:6-11:12. There are, however, sections addressed to Gentiles, e.g.,
11:13-24, and several balanced sentences showing how salvation
comes to both Jews and Gentiles, 1:16; 2:9f.; 2:14-24; 3:29f.; 11:25;
15:8-13.

3. The significance of God's wrath in Paul's thought cannot
be underestimated. Studies on Paul that concentrate on Justification, or Being in Christ, tend to side-step God's wrath. For an
early corrective of this tendency see E. Brunner, *The Letter to
the Romans*, 1959, 166-68.

4. E. P. Sanders convincingly argued this point in a presentation before an NEH seminar led by L. H. Feldman at Yeshiva

University in the summer of 1985. He will publish the evidence shortly.

5. Commentators who miss the irony in Paul's description of the self-satisfied Jew in Rom. 2:17-20 find themselves unable to give a coherent statement on Paul's attitude toward the law in Romans. The words "having in the law the embodiment of knowledge and truth" cannot be taken as Paul's own evaluation of the law, as done by most conservative exegetes, e.g., F. F. Bruce, *Paul: Apostle of the Heart Set Free*, 189.

6. H. Weiss, "How Can Jeremiah Compare the Migration of Birds to Knowledge of God's Justice?" *BR* II.3 (1986):42-45.

7. Philo and early Rabbis exercised their skills in order to prove that God rested on the Sabbath in accordance with Torah. Aristotelian logic and biblical exegesis were creatively combined in these efforts. H. L. Strack, P. Billerbeck, *Kommentar zum neuen Testament aus Talmud und Midrash*, ad John 5:17 (Exod. Rabb. 30:9) Philo, *De Cher.* 86-90; *Leg.* All. I. 5-6.

8. According to A. Heschel's felicitous phrase, righteousness is "God's stake in human history," *The Prophets*, 1962. I. 198.

9. For a review of the literature on the meaning of righteousness see J. A. Ziesler, *The Meaning of Righteousness in Paul*, 1970, 1-14. For understanding righteousness as having to do primarily with truthfulness and the keeping of promise see, S. K. Williams, "The Righteousness of God in Romans."

10. Faith is not a condition for righteousness but rather the very instrument by which God reveals his righteousness as he saves, see R. Bultmann, *Theology of the New Testament*, 1959, I. 314-16.

11. It is God's truthfulness and mercy that cause Him to exercise his righteousness rather than his wrath, Rom. 15:8f. Therefore men and women receive it as grace, as gift.

12. The central problem of the Adam/Christ analogy is the

paradoxical character of the relationship between the One and the Many, as K. Barth clearly saw, *Christ and Adam*, 1956. But this problem is solved if one recognizes the apocalyptic matrix of Paul's thought. Within it the eschatological act of salvation is just as universal as the original act of creation. See C. E. B. Cranfield, "On Some of the Problems in the Interpretation of Rom. 5:12."

13. With the words "God shows his love for us in that while we were yet sinners Christ died for us" (Rom. 5:8), Paul gives to the cross not only a creative role, which is emphasized by others who recognize the apocalpytic center of Paul's thought (e.g., E. Kasemann and J. C. Beker), but also a very significant revelational role as the manifestation of God's love.

14. J. C. Beker speaks of the "ontological 'cosmic'-apocalyptic significance" of the cross and the resurrection, *Paul the Apostle*, 194, and identifies the cross with the "eschatological judgement of the powers" (p. 190), and the resurrection with the inauguration of a "new ontological reality" (p. 196). He writes, "The shortcoming of a kerygmatic interpretation of the cross, such as Bultmann's, is in its inability to do justice to the resurrection as a historical-apocalyptic event" (p. 196).

15. See W. D. Davies, *The Torah in the Messianic age and/or the Age to Come*, 1952.

16. Philo, *Spec. Leg.*, *passim*; cp. Baruch 3:29f.

17. For the basic argument against the autobiographical interpretation of Romans 7, see W. G. Kümmel, *Romer 7 und die Bekehrung des Paulus*, 1929, and K. Stendahl, "The Apostle Paul and the Introspective Conscience of the West," in *Paul Among the Jews and Gentiles*, 1976, 78-96.

18. H. J. Schoeps' words are to the point: "In the great chapters 9-11 Paul sketches out a theology of saving history, for he strives to unfold God's plan in time and eternity," *Paul: The Theology of the Apostle in the Light of Jewish Religious History*, 1959, 235.

19. See A. G. Baxter and J. A. Ziesler, "Paul and Arboriculture: Romans 11: 17-24."

20. See A. Marmorstein, *The Doctrine of Merits in Old Rabbinic Literature*, 1968, 22-36.

21. Since Paul admits not to have been to Rome yet, it has been argued that this list of greetings should have belonged originally to another letter sent to one of his own churches. But if one recognizes the mobility of the urban masses within the Roman Empire, it would not be strange for Paul to know many people who at the time of the writing of Romans resided in Rome. The very fact that Paul knew of their presence there may have been an incentive to write in anticipation of a future journey, and the expectation of support for a future mission to Spain. Supporting this view see, K. Aland, "Der Schluss und die ursprüngliche Gestalt des Römerbriefes," *Neutestamentliche Entwurfe*, 1979, 284-301. Against this view see J. Knox, "Romans 15:14-33 and Paul's Conception of His Apostolic Mission."

22. For a review of the issue, see M. E. Boring, "The Language of Universal Salvation in Paul," *JBL* 105 (1986):269-92.

23. See W. A. Meeks, *The First Urban Christians: The Social World of the Apostle Paul*, 1983, 13-19. 3

Chapter IV

1. M. Hengel, *Crucifixion*, 1974, 1-10.

2. L. Diez Merino, "El suplicio de la cruz en la literatura judía intertestamental."

3. Hengel, *Crucifixion*, 4.

4. "What Was the Medical Cause of Christ's Death?" *Medical World News*, Oct. 21, 1966.

5. A rather trustworthy account of Paul's death may be read in the letter of Clement of Rome to the Corinthians (5:4-7). Legendary accounts developed soon after, e.g., in the *Acts of Paul*.

6. It is incomprehensible that resurrection and exaltation could by themselves have established messianic claims for Jesus after a totally unmessianic earthly life. This point is well argued by N. A. Dahl, *The Crucified Messiah, and other Essays*, 1974, 28-33.

7. On the question of Jesus' crucifixion see A. E. Harvey, *Jesus and the Constraints of History*, 1982, 11-35.

8. Beker's concern to emphasize that for Paul salvation is God's rather than Christ's doing is certainly on target, *Paul the Apostle, passim*.

9. Clearly the most difficult problem for the understanding of Paul is to establish in what way he saw continuity and discontinuity between Adam, Abraham, and Moses, on the one hand, and Christ, on the other. Paul is able to emphasize one or the other; thus his would-be interpreter never ceases to be puzzled. This is true both in terms of the history of the people and of the representative figures within it, and of the significance of the Torah as the depository of that history and its meaning for the people, which, in turn, needs to be read and interpreted.

10. This is to say that the cross and the resurrection are, like creation, historico-cosmic events. The preaching of the cross certainly actualizes the creative power of the cross, but it does not reduce the cross and the resurrection to faith events actual only in preaching.

11. See the description of the evidence in W. D. Davies, *Torah in the Messianic and/or the Age to Come*, 1952, 39-49.

12. In the *Apocalypse of Baruch and the Apocalypse of Ezra* there is an intervening period of time between the advent of Messiah and the general resurrection. See discussion of these passages in H. J. Schoeps, *Paul*, 42.

13. Even Bultmann recognizes this much, "Man Between the Times According to the New Testament."

14. This is clearly the case in Luke's selection of Isaiah 61 as the text for Jesus' sermon at Nazareth, Luke 4:16-21.

15. Josephus, *Antiquities*, XIV, 352-491.

16. For a detailed analysis of all references to the Parousia see W. Radl, *Ankunft des Herrn: zur Bedeutung und Function der Parousie-aussagen bei Paulus*, 1981.

17. As seen by Paul, "the rule of God competes historically with the dominion of sin, death, and law. The disarmed rulers still threaten with the power that unbelief concedes to them. For this reason even the believer is not yet free from the threat of the disarmed powers. . . . Thus he is guarded against any presumption of salvation." A. H. J. Gunneweg and W. Schmithals, *Authority*, 1982, 139.

18. "He experiences the divine address, which compels him to earthly pilgrimage. This fact makes him a historical being: he stands beneath the sign of exodus and his horizon is hope," E. Käsemann, *Perspectives on Paul*, 1971, 5.

19. For a description of Paul as an apocalypticist with messianic masochistic problems, see R. Rubinstein, *My Brother Paul, passim.*

20. See J. W. Drane, *Paul: Libertine or Legalist?*, 1975.

21. See J. Fletcher, *The New Morality*, 1966.

22. For an enlightening comparison of Paul's reference to a visit to the third heaven with reports of other Jewish visionaries, see G. G. Scholem, *Jewish Gnosticism, Merkabah Mysticism and Talmudic Tradition*, 1965, 14-19.

23. To borrow the sub-title and the main point, if not the argumentation, of J. C. Beker's *Paul the Apostle.*

Chapter V

1. To become acquainted with current scholarship on the question of Paul's understanding of the law, see H. Huebner, *Law in Paul's Thought*, 1984, 44-80; H. Räisänen, *Paul and the Law*, 1983; J. A. Sanders, "Torah and Paul"; E. P Sanders, *Paul, the Law, and the Jewish People*, 1983; W. D. Davies, "Paul and the Law: Reflections on Pitfalls in Interpretation;" U. Wilckens, "Zur Entwicklung des paulinischen Gesetz verstandniss," and L. Gaston, "Paul and the Torah." To the problem of Paul's understanding of the law three basic solutions seem to recommend themselves: (1) Paul contradicted himself (Räisänen, (2) Paul wrote to concrete local situations in the urgency of the moment and never made an effort to systematize his thoughts on the subject (Sanders), and (3) Paul went through a process of theological development; as his thought matured he abandoned previously held views (Huebner).

2. On the sense of conditional sentences in Paul, see M. Winger, "Unreal Conditions in the Letters of Paul."

3. W. Gutbrod, "NOMOS."

4. H. J. Schoeps' claim that Paul's understanding of the law was based on a misunderstanding of the role of the law in Judaism does not seem correct, *Paul*, 213-18.

5. H. H. Rowley, *The Biblical Doctrine of Election*, 1950, 15-44.

6. That the Jewish way of life for Philo allowed attendance at the gymnasium is clear from A. Mendelson, *Secular Education in Philo of Alexandria*, 1983.

7. In Rom. 10:6-8, Paul refers to Deut. 30:12-14 in order to establish that righteousness by faith was taught by Torah. Thus Christ is presented as both the Word of Torah, which Jews should listen to, and the Word of the Gospel, which is still near to them. Israel is therefore responsible for its own failure to hear. See J. A. Sanders, "Torah and Christ."

8. The glorification of Torah is one of the main themes in *The Book of Jubilees*, IV *Ezra*, and the *Letter of Aristeas*. The Torah is described as eternal in I Enoch 99:2; IV Ezra 9:28-37, as everlasting in *Jubilees* 33:17; *Pss Solomon* 10:5, and as imperishable in *Jubilees* 12; IV *Ezra* 9:37.

9. The Jewish discussion as to the possible superiority of some commandments over others is present in the hidden agenda of the test question put to Jesus by a lawyer in Matt. 22:36, "Master, which is the great commandment in the law?" See V. P. Furnish, *The Love Commandment in the New Testament*, 1972, 32.

10. For an impersonal interpretation of the elemental spirits of the world see A. J. Bandstra, *The Law and the Elements of the World*, 1964.

11. For a detailed argument see B. Reicke, "The Law and This World According to Paul. "

12. The autobiographical interpretation goes back to Origen, Augustine, and the Protestant Reformers. For the basic argument against it see above Ch. 3, n. 21.

13. Bultmann correctly observed that Paul does not speak much of the forgiveness of sin (which implies release from guilt). Paul rather speaks of release from sinning, acting under the power of sin, *Theology of the New Testament*, I. 287.

14. See J. C. Beker, *Paul the Apostle*, 238.

15. The first person references in Romans 7 are liturgical in origin and have their basis in the confessional Psalms and the language of prayer. Augustine's *Confessions* represent the best example of this genre in Christian literature.

16. The teleological meaning of the epigram "Christ is the end of the law" has been forcefully demonstrated on both philological and contextual grounds by R. D. Badenas, *Christ the End of the Law. Romans 10:4 in Pauline Perspective*, 1985. P. W. Meyer,

who also argues for the teleological meaning of *end in the text*, states that the law cannot be tied to the old aeon, but he fails to prove that there is no polarity in Paul between Christ and the law, "Romans 10:4 and the 'End' of the Law," 69. Whether *end* means "goal" or "abolition" makes no material difference in the meaning of the sentence as far as the law is concerned, since once the goal has been reached the purpose for the thing's existence is no longer operative. The choice of a meaning for *end* only affects the significance of Christ. The sentence intends to say something about Him, rather than about the law.

17. In E. Käsemann's words, "Obedience is the sign of regained creatureliness." *Perspectives on Paul*, 41.

18. For an early warning about the dangers encountered when building theological edifices with New Testament metaphors see A. Richardson, *An Introduction to the Theology of the New Testament*, 1958, 232-36.

19. On the notion of the ethical life as progress along stages on the road to virtue in Philo and the Stoics, see H. Weiss, "A Schema of the 'Road' in Philo and Lucan," *forthcoming* in *Studia Philonica*.

20. "Unlike the Stoics or Philo, he pays no tribute to the ideal of character-building, even in the life of the believer. Man is not under his own control. His salvation and his ruin depend on the Lord whom he serves." E. Käsemann, *Perspectives on Paul*, 29.

21. This eschatological tension is also analyzed in the universalistic, apocalyptic perspective of Paul by E. Käsemann, *Perspectives on Paul*, 16.3

Chapter VI

1. For the Platonic understanding of the soul's immortality see Phaedo, 64-68.

2. For the most elaborate presentation of this view see G. W. F. Hegel, *Phenomenology of Spirit.*

3. For modern studies on this point see J. A. T. Robinson, *The Body: A Study in Pauline Theology*, 1952, and R. Jewett, *Paul's Anthropological Terms: A Study of Their Use in Conflict Settings*, 1971. A notable exception is R. Gundry, *SOMA in Biblical Theology with Emphasis on Pauline Anthropology*, 1976, who argues that body plus mind embrace the human constitution.

4. E. Käsemann, *Perspectives on Paul*, 18-22, makes the point that heart is used by Paul to designate the center of human life and personal existence. In this way he empties the word "body" from any connotation of person or personality. Body or corporeality, then, connotes solidarity, co-humanity. Käsemann is arguing against Bultmann's understanding of body as the concreteness of the individual person, *Theology of the New Testament*, I. 195-97.

5. For the Stoic use of these terms see J.M. Rist, *Stoic Philosophy*, 1969, 256-72.

6. See O. Cullmann, "Immortality of the Soul or Resurrection of the Dead," 36-54.

7. For a reconstruction of the Corinthians' understanding of the Gospel, see W. Schmithals, *Gnosticism in Corinth*, 1971.

8. For a different understanding of the three possible "bodies" see J. C. Beker, *Paul the Apostle*, 288. Beker designates life in "the era of Christ" as life in a "mortal body." This makes him then exegete Phil. 1:10 as stating that "Paul appeals for the blameless state of the body at the Parousia" on an individualistic basis, which seems far from the apostle's mind. More to the point

is Käsemann's observation that the notion of the body retains structural characteristics with the exalted Lord, making possible the incorporation of believers into it, *Perspectives on Paul*, 104.

9. In this scenario the concept of the body clearly informs Paul's advice: the Christian is a member of the body that died for the salvation of unbelievers.

10. The cultic background of meals held by adherents to the mystery cults is described by A.D. Nock, *Early Gentile Christianity and Its Hellenistic Background*, 1964, 72-76.

11. It is not at all correct to say that "in 8:10f. he (Paul) urges the general waiver of a right which he himself would not contest, the right to participate in temple meals with the appropriate mental reservations," G. Theissen, *The Social Setting of Pauline Christianity: Essays on Corinth*, 1982, 122.   According to Paul, Christians must always act with a mind that is fully convinced of the rightness of their actions before God and before mankind.   In an effort to recreate the conditions of the Corinthian church, Theissen interprets Paul's words without any reference to the key role played by the concept of the body or to his warnings about immorality and idolatry, as exemplified by the story of the wilderness wanderings.

12. Blinded by his translation of the "weak" and the "strong" as the "poor" and the "rich", Theissen suggests that the discernment of the body has to do with the differentiation of the eucharistic bread from animal meat which only the rich could afford! *Social Setting of Pauline Christianity*, 153, 159.

13.   The Corinthians are abusing both the eucharist and baptism because of their failure to see the concreteness of their life on earth.   The notion of the body of Christ argues for the actuality of the Christian presence in a fallen world.   As stated by Käsemann "He (Paul) puts the main stress of the eucharist on the remembrance of, and participation in, Jesus' death and expressly denies that baptism, in which we die with Christ, also allows us to participate in his resurrection.   It merely gives us the *expectation and hope* of the resurrection," *Perspectives on Paul*, 58.   Thus

Christians living as the body of Christ on earth should not make themselves members of other bodies.

14. At the time of Paul's missionary activities the church had not yet become an ecclesiastical institution. When Paul uses the word church he refers to the local congregations scattered throughout the Roman Empire. Still all Christians are one body. How is this to be understood is difficult to determine. For a "realistic" interpretation see J. A. T. Robinson, *The Body*. For a "metaphorical" interpretation see E. Best, *One Body in Christ*, 1955.

15. As R. Jewett correctly argues, it is from this basic premise that the apostle takes a tolerant attitude toward the views of others, *Christian Tolerance: Paul's Message to the Modern Church*, 1982, 33.

16. As argued by V. Branick, Paul associates the pneumatic existence of the Christian community with a Christian mentality that achieves community peace, "Source and Redaction Analysis of I. Cor. 1-3."

Chapter VII

1. N. Schneider, *Die rhetorische Eigenart der paulinischen Antithese*. Tübingen, 1970, 19.

2. E. Schweizer, "PNEUMA, PNEUMATIKOS."

3. John 3:7f.

4. This warfare between the flesh and the spirit may be understood in the light of the Pharisaic doctrine of the two spirits, or impulses, within individuals. One urges toward good while the other toward evil. See W. D. Davies, *Paul and Rabbinic Judaism*, 1970, 20-29. In Paul, however, the flesh and the spirit are not just

just anthropological concepts. They are also cosmic-eschatological categories.

5. That Paul did not build, or even intend to build an ethical system has become a commonplace in current studies of Pauline ethics. See W. Schrage, *Die konkreten Einzelgebote im der paulinischen Paraenese: Ein Beitrage zur neuentestamentlichen Ethik*, 1969, 123.

6. On the intricacies of this problem see W. A. Meeks, "Since Then You Would Need to be Out of the World."

7. See P. Perkins, "Paul and Ethics."

8. A point emphasized by R. Bultmann, *The Old and New Man*, 1967, 29f.

9. The text is, admittedly, difficult to interpret. For a discussion of the difficulties see A. T. Hanson, "The Midrash in II Cor. 3: A Reconsideration."

10. See R. Schnackenburg, "Christian Adulthood According to St. Paul."

11. P. W. Meyer makes an important distinction against a hermeneutical tradition endorsed by Augustine and Luther. According to them the power of the Spirit enables men and women to love God and so fulfill the law. In that case God's gift demonstrates God's love and sustains the Christian's life. But the power of the Spirit can also be seen as a supernatural, transforming power that enables the recipient to lead a transcendent life, "The Holy Spirit in the Pauline Letters: A Contextual Exploration."

12. As V. Furnish concedes there is no "support for the hypothesis that he (Paul) conceived of the traditional words of Jesus as constituting a new Torah or a Christian Halakah," *Theology and Ethics in Paul*, 1968, 65. See also his Appendix, "A Survey of Nineteenth-and-Twentieth-Century Interpretations of Paul's Ethic," 242-79.

13. See A. Nygren, *Agape and Eros*, 1953, 116. Here Paul is in marked contrast with the moralists of his time who understood love to be motivated by humanitarian considerations. See Plutarch, *Moralia*, 478-92.

14. The relationship of faith and love in Paul is tied to the concept of obedience. God demonstrated his love at the cross of Jesus. This elicits the human response of faith. But faith is obedience, and obedience is love, Nygren, *Agape and Eros*, 124-26. Christian conduct is a demonstration of God's love in as much as it actualizes the once-for-all conduct of Christ on the cross.

15. Theologies of liberation attempt to replace the view of love as self-sacrificing with a view of love as self-assertive. But theologies of liberation tend to forget the demands that the Pauline doctrine of obedience places on all Christians.

16. For love as the re-uniting of those estranged see P. Tillich, *Love, Power and Justice; Ontological Analyses and Ethical Applications*, New York: Oxford, 1964, 115-25.

17. It is characteristic of theologies of perfection to define perfection in reference to the law and to think of the teaching of Jesus as a new law, or a new halacha, Matthew 5:48. But Paul thinks of perfection in reference to the completeness of God's power to accomplish his purpose to save.

Chapter VIII

1. For an understanding of the contemporary notion that men and women lived as slaves of divinities see Petronius, *Satyricon.*

2. R. F. Hock, "The Workshop as Social Setting for Paul's Missionary Preaching," and *The Social Context of Paul's Ministry: Tentmaking and Apostleship*, 42-47.

3. W. Bousset, *Kyrios Christos*, 1913.

4. P. W. Meyer argues against the notion that "for Paul the Christian has been transported into 'the age to come.' Paul nowhere makes such a claim, and his attachment to the so-called 'doctrine of the two ages' is too loose to allow us to infer the claim from what he does say," "The Holy Spirit in the Pauline Letters," p. 14, n. 13. We have not argued, however, that Paul thinks that Christians have been transported to the age to come, see Ch. VI, n. 13. We have consistently argued for the eschatological tension between the "already" and the "not yet." Paul has used the apocalyptic pattern of the doctrine of the two ages in order to explain the significance of the cross and the resurrection of Jesus Christ. Meyer himself argues that what Paul says about the Spirit is taken from his heritage but given a distinctly Christian sense by the way he connects it with what is essentially Christian. The same is true about Paul's apocalpytic vision.

5. For a clear presentation of this point see G. G. Collins, "Power Made Perfect in Weakness: 2 Cor. 12:9, 10."

6. See R. A. Johnson, *The Vitality of the Individual in the Thought of Ancient Israel*, 1964, 95-109.

7. "For Paul the only valid and visible sign of apostolicity was the weakness the apostle was prepared to accept in order to allow the power of Christ's cross to be manifest in him," C. K. Barrett, *A Commentary on the Second Epistle to the Corinthians*, New York: Harper, 1973, 312.

8. It must be clear at all times that what the power of God perfects is not the weakness of the flesh, but the weakness of the cross in which the flesh of Christians has been crucified.

9. For different assessments of Paul's understanding of the nature and authority of an apostle, see W. Schmithals, *The Office of Apostle in the Early Church*, 1969, and J. H. Schultz, *Paul and the Anatomy of Apostolic Authority*, 1975.

10. It is quite clear that in II Cor. 3 Paul's words are based on a homily on Exodus 34, and that he is making a contrast between the restrictions imposed by God, who is remote in an unapproachable mountain top, and the Spirit, who is now among humans and by His very presence provides the freedom that is appropriately His. See C. F. D. Moule, "2 Cor. 3:18b, Kathaper Apo Kyriou Pneumatos."

BIBLIOGRAPHY OF WORKS CITED

Abbreviations

BA	Biblical Archaeologist
BR	Bible Review
BTh	Biblical Theology
CBQ	Catholic Biblical Quarterly
DOP	Dumbarton Oaks Papers
Int	Interpretation
JBL	Journal of Biblical Literature
JournStudNT	Journal for the Study of the New Testament
NovTest	Novum Testamentum
NTS	New Testament Studies
SBT	Studia Biblica Franciscana
ScJTh	Scottish Journal of Theology
TDNT	Kittel's Theological Dictionary of the New Testament
ZAW	Zeitschrift für altestamentliche Wissenschaft
ZNW	Zeitschrift für neuentestamentliche Wissenschaft

Aland, K. "Der Schluss und die ursprüngliche Gestalt des Römerbriefes, in *Neutestamentlich Entwurfe*. Munich: Kaiser. 1979.

Bacon, B. W. *The Story of St. Paul*. New York: Houghton Mifflin. 1904.

Badenas, R. *Christ the End of the Law: Romans 10:4 in Pauline Perspective*. Sheffield: JSOT. 1985.

Bandstra, A. J. *The Law and the Elements of the World*. Kampen: Kok. 1964.

Barrett, C. K. *Essays on Paul*. Philadelphia: Westminster. 1982.

_____. "Paul and the 'Pilar Apostles'," in J. N. Sevenster and W. van Unnik (eds.). *Studia Paulina*. Harlem: 1953.

Barth, K. *Christ and Adam*. New York: Macmillan. 1956.

Baur, F. C. *Paul: The Apostle of Jesus Christ*. 2 volumes. Edingurgh: T. T. Clark. 1886 (German original, 1845).

Baxter, A. G., and J. A. Ziesler, "Paul and Arboriculture: Romans 11: 17-24," *JournStudNT* 24 (1985) 25-32.

Beker, J. C. *Paul the Apostle: The Triumph of God in Life and Thought*. Philadelphia: Fortress. 1980.

Best, E. *One Body in Christ*. London: SPCK. 1955.

Betz, H. D. *Der Apostel Paulus und die sokratische Tradition*. Tubingen: Mohr. 1972.

Blenkinsopp, J. *Prophecy and Canon*. Notre Dame: University of Notre Dame Press. 1977.

Bornkamm, G. *Paul*. New York: Harper. 1971.

Bousset, W. *Kyrios Christos: A History of the Belief in Christ from the Beginnings of Christianity to Irenaeus.* Nashville: Abingdon. 1970 (German original, 1913).

Bowers, P. "Paul and Religious Propaganda in the First Century," *NovTest* 22 (1980) 316-23.

Branick, V. P. "Source and Redaction Analysis of I Cor. 1-3," *JBL* 101 (1982) 251-69.

Bruce, F. F. *Men and Movements in the Primitive Church.* Exeter: Paternoster. 1979.

_____. *Paul: Apostle of the Heart Set Free.* Grand Rapids: Eerdmans. 1977.

Brunner, E. *The Letter to the Romans.* Philadelphia: Westminster. 1959.

Bultmann, R. "Man Between the Times According to the New Testament," in S. Ogden (ed.). *Existence and Faith.* New York: Meridian. 1960.

_____. *The Old and New Man.* Atlanta: John Knox. 1967.

_____. *Theology of the New Testament.* 2 volumes. New York: Scribner. 1959.

Campbell, W. S. "Some Recent Literature on Paul's Letter to the Romans: A Critical Survey," *BTh* 25 (1975) 25-34.

Collins, G. G. "Power Made Perfect in Weakness: 2 Cor. 12:9, 10," *CBQ* 33 (1971) 528-37.

Conzelmann, H. *The Theology of St.* Luke. London: Faber and Faber. 1961.

Cranfield, C. E. B. "On Some of the Problems in the Interpretation of Rom. 5:12," *ScJTh* 22 (1969) 324-41.

Cullmann, O. "Immortality of the Soul or Resurrection of the Dead," in K. Stendahl (ed.). *Immortality and Resurrection*. New York: Macmillan. 1965.

Dahl, N. A. *The Crucified Messiah and Other Essays*. Minneapolis: Augsburg. 1974.

Davies, W. D. *Paul and Rabbinic Judaism*. London: SPCK. 1970.

_____. "Paul and the Law: Reflections on Pitfalls in Interpretation," in M. D. Hooker, and S. G. Wilson (eds.). *Paul and Paulinism: Essays in Honor of C. K. Barrett*. London: SPCK. 1982.

_____. *The Torah in the Messianic Age and/or the Age to Come*. Philadelphia: Society of Biblical Literature. 1952.

Deissmann, A. *Paul: A Study in Social and Religious History*. New York: Harper. 1912.

Diez Merino, L. "El suplicio de la cruz en la literatura judía intertestamental," *SBF* 26 (1976) 31-120.

Dodd, C. H. *The Bible and the Greeks*. London: Hodder and Stoughton. 1935.

Drane, J. W. *Paul: Libertine or Legalist?* London: SPCK. 1975.

Dunn, J. D. G. *Unity and Diversity in The New Testament*. Philadelphia: Westminster. 1977.

Feine, P.; J. Behm; and W. G. Kümmel. *Introduction to the New Testament*. Nashville: Abingdon. 1966.

Finegan, J. *The Archaeology of the New Testament*. Princeton: Princeton University Press. 1969.

Fletcher, J. *The New Morality*. Philadelphia: Westminster. 1966.

Fuller, R. H. *The Foundations of New Testament Christology.* New York: Scribner. 1965.

Furnish, V. P. *The Love Commandment in the New Testament.* Nashville: Abingdon. 1972.

_____. *Theology and Ethics in Paul.* Nashville: Abingdon. 1968.

Gaston, L. "Paul and the Torah," in A. Davies (ed.). *Antisemitism, and the Foundations of Christianity.* New York: Paulist. 1979.

Gundry, R. *SOMA in Biblical Theology with Emphasis on Pauline Anthropology.* Cambridge: Cambridge University Press. 1976.

Gunneweg, A. H. J., and W. Schmithals. *Authority.* Nashville: Abingdon. 1982.

Gutbrod, W. "NOMOS," *TDNT.* VI. 1069-78.

Habel, N. "The Form and Significance of the Call Narrative," *ZAW* 77 (1965) 297-323.

Haenchen, E. *The Acts of the Apostles: A Commentary.* Philadelphia: Fortress. 1971.

Hahn, F. *The Titles of Jesus in Christology.* New York: World. 1969.

Hanson, A. T. "The Midrash in II Cor. 3: A Reconsideration," *JournStudNT* 9 (1980) 1-20.

Hengel, M. *Crucifixion.* Philadelphia: Fortress. 1974.

_____. *The Charismatic Leader and His Followers.* New York: Crossroads. 1981.

Heschel, A. *The Prophets.* 2 volumes. New York: Harper. 1962.

Hock, R. "Paul's Tent Making and the Problem of his Social Class," *JBL* 97 (1978) 555-64.

_____. *The Social Context of Paul's Ministry: Tent Making and Apostleship.* Philadelphia: Fortress. 1980.

_____. "The Workshop as Social Setting for Paul's Missionary Preaching," *CBQ* 41 (1979) 438-50.

Huebner, H. *Law in Paul's Thought.* Edinburgh: T. T. Clark. 1984.

Hugedé, N. *St Paul et la culture grècque.* Geneva: Labor et Fides. 1966.

Hultgren, A. "Paul's Pre-Christian Perceptions of the Church: Their Purpose and Nature," *JBL* 95 (1976) 97-111.

Jewett, R. *A Chronology of Paul's Life.* Philadelphia: Fortress. 1979.

_____. "Major Impulses in the Theological Interpretation of Romans since Barth," *Int* 34 (1980) 17-31.

_____. *Paul's Anthropological Terms: A Study of Their Use in Conflict Settings.* Leiden: Brill. 1971.

_____. *Christian Tolerance: Paul's Message to the Modern Church.* Philadelphia: Westminster. 1982.

Johnson, R. A. *The Vitality of the Individual in the Thought of Ancient Israel.* Cardiff: University of Wales Press. 1964.

Kantorowicz, E. H. "The Baptism of the Apostles," *DOP* 9 (1955) 201-51.

Käsemann. E. *Perspectives on Paul.* Philadelphia: Fortress. 1971.

Knox, J. "Romans 15:14-33 and Paul's Conception of His Apostolic Mission," *JBL* 83 (1964) 1-11.

Kümmel, W. G. *Römer 7 und die Bekehrung des Paulus.* Leipzig: Heinrichs. 1929.

Ludemann, G. *Paul, Apostle to the Gentiles: Studies in Chronology.* Philadelphia: Fortress. 1984.

MacDonald, D. R. *The Legend and the Apostle: The Battle for Paul in Story and Canon.* Philadelphia: Westminster. 1983.

Mainhardus, O. F. A. "Paul's Missionary Journey to Spain: Tradition and Folklore," *BA* 41 (1978) 61-63.

Marmorstein, A. *The Doctrine of Merits in Old Rabbinic Literature.* New York: KTAV. 1968.

Meeks, W. A. "Since Then You Would Need to be Out of the World," in T. J. Ryan (ed.). *Critical History and Biblical Faith.* Villanova: College Theology Society. 1979.

_____. *The First Urban Christians: The Social World of the Apostle Paul.* New Heaven: Yale University Press. 1983.

Mendelson, A. "A Re-Appraisal of Wolfson's Method," *Studia Philonica* 3 (1974-5) 11-26.

_____. *Secular Education in Philo of Alexandria.* Cincinnati: Hebrew Union College. 1983.

Meyer, P. W. "Romans 10:4 and the 'End' of the Law," in J. L. Crenshaw, and S. Sandmel (eds.). *The Divine Helmsman.* New York: KTAV. 1980.

_____. "The Holy Spirit in the Pauline Letters: A Contextual Exploration," *Int* 33 (1979) 3-18.

Minear, P. S. "Dear Theo: The Kerygmatic Intention and Claim of the Book of Acts," *Int 27(1973) 131-50.*

Moule, C. D. F. "2 Cor. 3:18b, Kathaper Apo Kyriou Pneumatos," in *Neues Testament und Geschichte: Historisches Geschehen und Deutung im Neuen Testament.* Tubingen: Mohr. 1972. pp. 231-37.

Nickle, K. F. *The Collection: A Study in Paul's Strategy.* Naperville: Allenson. 1966.

Nock, A. D. *Early Gentile Christianity and its Hellenistic Background.* New York: Harper. 1964.

_____. *St. Paul.* New York: Harper. 1963.

Nygren, A. *Agape and Eros.* Philadelphia: Westminster. 1953.

Pagels, E. *The Gnostic Paul: Gnostic Exegesis of the Pauline Letters.* Philadelphia: Fortress. 1975.

Perkins, P. "Paul and Ethics," *Int* 38 (1984) 268-80.

Perrin, N. *The New Testament: An Introduction.* New York: Harcourt, Brace, Jovanovich. 1974.

Rad, G. von. *Old Testament Theology.* 2 volumes. New York: Harper. 1965.

Radl, W. *Ankunft des Herrn: zur Bedeutung und Function der Parousie-aussagen bei Paulus.* Frankfurt: Lang. 1981.

Räisänen, H. *Paul and the Law.* Tubingen: Mohr. 1983.

Reicke, B. "The Law and This World According to Paul," *JBL* 70 (1951) 259-76.

Richardson, A. *An Introduction to the Theology of the New Testament.* New York: Harper. 1958.

Rist, J. M. *Stoic Philosophy.* Cambridge: Cambridge University Press. 1969.

Robinson, J. A. T. *The Body: A Study in Pauline Theology.* London: SCM. 1952.

Rowley, H. H. *The Biblical Doctrine of Election*. London: Lutter-worth. 1950.

Rubinstein, R. *My Brother Paul*. New York: Harper. 1972.

Sanders, E. P. *Paul and Palestinian Judaism*. Philadelphia: Fortress. 1978.

_____. *Paul, the Law, and the Jewish People*. Philadelphia: Fortress. 1983.

Sanders, J. A. "Torah and Christ," *Int* 29 (1975) 370-90.

_____. "Torah and Paul," in J. Jervell and W. A. Meeks (eds.). *God's Christ and His People*. Oslo: Universities Forlaget. 1977.

Sanders, J. T. "The Salvation of the Jews in Luke Acts," in C. H. Talbert (ed.). *Luke-Acts: New Perspectives from the Society of Biblical Literature Seminar*. New York: Crossroads. 1984. pp. 104-128.

Schmithals, W. *Gnosticism in Corinth*. Nashville: Abingdon. 1971.

_____. *The Office of Apostle in the Early Church*. Nashville: Abingdon. 1969.

Schnackenburg, R. "Christian Adulthood According to St. Paul," *CBQ* 25 (1963) 354-70.

Schoeps, H. J. *Paul: The Theology of the Apostle in the Light of Jewish Religious History*. Philadelphia: Westminster. 1959.

Scholem, G. G. *Jewish Gnosticism, Merkabah Mysticism and Talmudic Tradition*. New York: Jewish Theological Seminary of America. 1965.

Schrage, W. *Die konkreten Einzelgebote im der paulinischen Paraenese: Ein Beitrage zur neuentestamentlichen Ethik*. Gütersloh: Mohn. 1969.

Schultz, J. H. *Paul and the Anatomy of Apostolic Authority.* Cambridge: Cambridge University Press. 1975.

Schweizer, E. "PNEUMA, PNEUMATIKOS," *TDNT.* VI. 415-27.

_____. "Traditional Ethical Patterns in the Pauline and Post-Pauline Letters and their Development," in E. Best and R. McL. Wilson (eds.). *Text and Interpretation.* Cambridge: Cambridge University Press. 1979. pp. 195-209.

Schweitzer, A. *The Mysticism of Paul.* New York: Seabury. 1931.

Smith, M. "The Reason for the Persecution of Paul and the Obscurity of Acts," in E. E. Urbach, R. J. Zwiserblowsky, and Ch. Wirszubski (eds.). *Studies in Mysticism and Religion.* Jerusalem: Magnus. 1967. pp. 261-68.

_____. "What Is Implied by the Variety of Messianic Figures," *JBL* 78 (1959) 66-72.

Spivey, R and D. M. Smith. *Anatomy of the New Testament.* New York: Macmillan. Second edition, 1974.

Stendahl, K. *Paul Among the Jews and Gentiles.* Philadelphia: Fortress. 1976.

Stowers, S. K. "Social Status, Public Speaking and Private Teaching: The Circumstances of Paul's Preaching Activity," *NovTest* 26 (1984) 59-82.

Strack, H. L., and P. Billerbeck. *Kommentar zum neuen Testament aus Talmud und Midrash.* Munich: Beck. 1922.

Talbert, C. H. "Promise and Fulfillment in Lucan Theology," in C. H. Talbert (ed.). *Luke-Acts: New Perspectives from the Society of Biblical Literature Seminar.* New York: Crossroads. 1984. pp. 91-103.

Tcherikover, V. *Hellenistic Civilization and the Jews.* Philadelphia: Jewish Publication Society. 1959.

Theissen, G. *The Social Setting of Pauline Christianity: Essays on Corinth.* Philadelphia: Fortress. 1982.

Unnik, W. C. van. *Tarsus or Jerusalem: The City of Paul's Youth.* London: Epworth. 1962.

Vermes, G. *Jesus the Jew: A Historian's Reading of the Gospel.* New York: Macmillan. 1973.

Weiss, J. *Earliest Christianity.* 2 volumes. New York: Harper. 1959.

Wilckens, W. "Zur Entwicklung des paulinischen Gesetz verstandniss," *NTS* 28 (1982) 154-90.

Wilcox, M. "'Upon the Tree'--Deut. 21:22-23 in the New Testament," *JBL* 96 (1977) 85-99.

Williams, S. K. "The Righteousness of God in Romans," *JBL* 99 (1980) 241-90.

Winger, M. "Unreal Conditions in the Letters of Paul," *JBL* 105 (1986) 110-12.

Wolfson, H. *Philo.* 2 volumes. Cambridge: Harvard University Press. 1948.

Ziesler, J. A. *The Meaning of Righteousness in Paul.* Cambridge: Cambridge University Press. 1970.

SUBJECT INDEX